True Companion

true companion

Thoughts on Being a Pastor's Wife

NANCY WILSON

canonpress
Moscow, Idaho

Published by Canon Press
P.O. Box 8729, Moscow, ID 83843
800.488.2034 | www.canonpress.com

Nancy Wilson, *True Companion:*
Thoughts on Being a Pastor's Wife
Copyright © 2013 by Nancy Wilson.

Cover design by Rachel Rosales.
Interior by Laura Storm Design.
Printed in the United States of America.

Library of Congress Cataloging-in-Publication Data
Wilson, Nancy, 1952-
  True companion : thoughts on being a pastor's wife / Nancy Wilson.
    pages cm
  ISBN 1-59128-129-6
  1. Spouses of clergy. I. Title.
  BV4395.W57 2013
  253'.22--dc23
                                    2012049499
13 14 15 16 17 18 19 20   10 9 8 7 6 5 4 3 2 1

To Mary Lou Busby,
a long-time friend
and faithful pastor's wife.

contents

preface   9
introduction   13

PART I · YOUR MARRIAGE

1	Your Husband's Helper	17
2	Loyalty	23
3	Stumbling the Minister	31
4	Flying Solo	37
5	Praying for the Pastor	41

PART 2 · YOUR CHILDREN

6	The Congregation at Home	49
7	Qualifications	55
8	First Principles	57

PART 3 · CHURCH DUTIES

9	The New Pastor's Wife	65
10	Your Relationship to the Church	71
11	Expectations for the Minister's Wife	79
12	Sunday Morning	85
13	Preparing for the Lord's Day	87

14 Bearing Burdens or Heavy Lifting   93
15 Cheerleading or Keeping Perspective   97
16 Counseling in the Church   101
17 Women's Ministry in the Church   109
18 The Benefits   113

PART 4 · CHALLENGES & TRIALS

19 When the Minister Needs Help   119
20 When Friends Leave   123
21 Friendships   129
22 Thick Skin   135
23 Vulnerability   145
24 Hospitality   151
25 Self-Evaluation   157

AN AUTOBIOGRAPHICAL NOTE

Before we get started talking about what it means to be married to a pastor, I need to introduce myself.

First I have to tell you that it never occurred to me that I might marry a minister. I was converted in college, and I had never known a minister's wife in all my life. I remember well the pastor of the church I attended with my family in high school, but I have no recollection of his wife. I'm not sure I ever thought of him as a family man at all. He just appeared in the pulpit in his black robe each week.

When Doug and I got married in 1975, he was pursuing his college degree after spending four years in the US Navy (submarine service). We imagined that after he finished (he got a masters in philosophy), we would be involved in some kind of Christian work. Doug grew up in a Christian home, and his father, a gifted evangelist, had started non-profit evangelistic bookstores in college towns. We assumed we might end up doing something very similar. We had both spent time working in his local bookstore, and I had been part-time staff for Inter-Varsity.

Our church was founded just a few months before our marriage in 1975. We were enthusiastic supporters, but it never dawned on us that in a very short time Doug would himself be the pastor. About a year and a half into it, our pastor announced that it was his last Sunday. He wished us all good luck and said something about how we should do whatever the Lord led us to do.

We didn't have any elders. I don't think we even had a statement of faith. But we had about thirty to fifty people, mostly very young like we were, and my husband had the guitar up front leading the singing. So there we were.

We tried to find someone else to take over as the pastor, but it soon became clear that God was calling my husband to do this thing. He didn't want to. I didn't want him to. It seemed impossible. All I knew was that I didn't want to be a pastor's wife. How's that for a glamorous beginning? There was no time for seminary training. My husband had to train on the job, and so did I.

This book is the result of a little newsletter for ministers' wives that I started a few years back. I believe that most women in this role feel a little inadequate, and it may be nice to know that you're not the only one. So if this book seems chatty, it's because I have gathered up some of those old newsletters to use here. And if I sound motherly, it's because my husband has been a minister now for over three decades, and I have a silver mine growing in my hair.

So welcome to my random thoughts about being a pastor's wife. I hope and pray that this will encourage you to see the significance and joy of your calling.

SO YOUR HUSBAND IS A

MINISTER

"So your husband is a minister!" That comment can conjure up all kinds of stereotypical ideas. It did for me. I had no idea what a minister's wife was supposed to do. I assumed she probably had to play the piano and wear a beehive hairdo. Or at least she would have to be in the choir. None of those things were possibilities for me, and I don't know what I was worried about because our church had neither a piano nor a choir at the time. Even so, I felt very intimidated at the idea of being the woman who was married to the minister. I was still in my twenties, and I didn't want to start wearing pumps and matronly dresses. Well, that was hardly a worry since my husband was preaching in his jeans back then (it was the 70's after all), and I was wearing long, flowy dresses to match my long, flowy hair. So you see, all my fears were ungrounded.

But what about everyone else's expectations? What would they expect me to be? We lived in a very small, old apartment. How could we host Bible studies and church meetings? Would I be expected to organize Sunday school or have everyone to dinner? Would everyone be looking at me? Would I ever see my husband? Would he ever get a day off?

About this time I spoke with my very jolly friend Mary Lou whose husband was a new minister. I told her all my concerns and she reassured me that I wouldn't have to play the piano or be up front. She described herself as a "behind the scenes" pastor's wife, and I thought that sounded perfect for me.

The thing that really settled my heart and mind was realizing that God would equip us both to do whatever He called us to do. I didn't have any worries about whether my husband was up to it. All my doubts had to do with me. The great relief came when I realized I would still simply be *Doug's wife*. That was something I had been doing for a couple of years already, and though I was no expert, at least it was familiar territory. In fact, I liked it. So even though my husband was taking on new responsibilities, my primary responsibilities would remain the same. I would still be my husband's helper, with no fancy titles, and that sounded reasonable enough.

So let's start there.

PART I

Your Marriage

chapter 1

YOUR HUSBAND'S

HELPER

Since a pastor's wife is still first and foremost *a wife*, she can consider her calling to be very similar to every other wife's calling: she is designed to be a helper. She takes care of her man. Nevertheless, this obvious first duty is the one that can sometimes get obscured and overlooked in the midst of family life and church business. We can get distracted by everyone else's pressing needs and neglect the weighty matter of our own marriage duties. Children have varying needs of their own, and the house is a lot to keep up with. Then there are the calls and interruptions common in many households. So how can any wife manage all this and still keep her husband and his needs from being relegated to obscurity? And what are his needs anyway? Who takes care of him? Surprise answer: you do!

Every wife should appreciate her husband's calling, and the minister's wife is no exception. Though I didn't expect (or want) Doug to become a minister, it was not because I had a low view of what it would take. It was actually the opposite. Even so, in the day-to-day, year-after-year labors, it is possible to forget that being married to a minister is a unique calling and a great honor. So a wife should maintain a high view of her husband's calling and gifts. A minister is called to shepherd a portion of God's flock, and this is a job that requires much self-sacrifice and patience. I don't have to tell you this, because no one knows this better than the minister's wife. She sees behind the scenes like no one else.

No wonder his batteries need recharging, and the minister's wife should recognize that she is God's primary means to do the recharging. Like any husband, he needs rest, he needs food, and he needs the restorative pleasures of the marriage bed. All these things she should "gift him" as a centerpiece of her own ministry to him. She should view these duties by faith, trusting that God will use them all to bless and strengthen her husband.

A good marriage is a comfort and an inestimable blessing. A minister with a healthy, happy marriage will be far more effective in his calling than if his marriage is anemic or strained. So consider the state of your marriage. Is it thriving? Is it in a slump? What can you do to improve things? God said it was not good for the man to be alone, so do all in your power, by God's grace, to make this true in your own marriage. You don't want him sighing with relief when he heads out the door in the morning. Even a good marriage can be better, so ask God to enrich and deepen your attachment to one another.

Wives are to respect their husbands. How's that going at your house? You may think it's going well and fine, but does he agree? Does your husband feel respected and honored?

Do you do what he says? Remember that vow about "love, honor, and obey"? So consider tuning things up. What has he asked you to do that you haven't yet done? Are you letting things slide or cutting corners and not telling him? Are you open and honest with him about everything? Does he know about that charge on the credit card? Are you quick to do what he asks? Do you keep confidences?

Evaluate

One of the first principles of marriage is to stay in fellowship with one another. That requires diligence and humility. You are Christians, so you know what to do: you mess up, you seek forgiveness. And you don't wait until tomorrow—you do it now. Doug and I call this keeping short accounts. If you let sins go by without confession and forgiveness, resentments will pile up and put distance between you. So the first duty is to stay in close fellowship. That keeps you from drifting apart and is a tremendous protection for your marriage.

I hope to be (though it doesn't sound like a flattering description at first) a "low maintenance" wife or a "two-bucket woman." (A two-bucket woman is one who can carry two buckets instead of just one . . . in other words, a strong woman.) That means I want to do my job without a lot of oversight and coaching, which frees my husband to do his job. Though we all have times when we need to pour out our troubles to our husbands, we ought to try to be the kind of wives who don't need that kind of attention *every single day*. It would be unrealistic (and maybe even unnatural) to be the kind of wife who never had a problem, but neither do we want to be his last counseling appointment each and every day. In other words, we want to be applying what we are learning and asking God to enable us to grow in grace so we are a positive help and not a drain on our husbands. He should have confidence that he is coming home to a woman who has her tasks in hand.

Most ministers (and often their wives) are involved in marriage counseling, and that is only possible if they have healthy marriages themselves. You can't fake it. And though ministers are not exempt from all the temptations and trials that everyone else faces, he has to live out the standards he preaches. He can't do this alone. His wife has got to be on board and willing to work hard on keeping the relationship in good shape.

Doug and I have seen marriages that seemed to be okay for twenty or twenty-five years suddenly tank. The crisis usually brings things to light that should have been addressed long ago, but they've been festering underground. The harvest finally comes in, and there it is in plain sight. So don't let things drift. Address your issues as they come up. If the relationship is neglected, it will eventually get sick. Gardens grow weeds and marriages do too. That's why they need to be tended.

Just imagine what would happen to our country if all the pulpits were filled with godly men who were unashamedly proclaiming God's Word. Men like this need wives who are preparing for them, making their homes places where the family can thrive in an atmosphere of love, affection, and respect.

I'm not saying that the state of the marriage is up to you. Husbands are ultimately responsible for the state of their families. But we wives have far more power than we realize to affect the atmosphere in our homes. We can make it one of peace and happiness. That's what I'm talking about. This is our privilege and our joy.

chapter 2

LOYALTY

All that the Bible teaches about women applies to Christian women in general, and not just to ministers' wives. But if we are to be helping the women in the congregation to obey God's Word, then we have to be doing it ourselves first, obviously. So all I say here is true for all wives, though I am making special application to the minister's wife.

First of all, she has to be the kind of woman who believes the Bible is true and submits to it in every area of her life. No exceptions. This means she is loyal to God first, and then to her husband and family, church and congregation.

A loyal wife is a security for her husband. "The heart of her husband safely trusts her; so he will have no lack of gain. She does him good and not evil all the days of her life" (Prov. 31:11–12). Loyalty to your husband means that you are a die-hard, one-man woman. It means you are faithful, constant, and true. You don't change, you don't yield (to the wrong suggestions), and you are not shaken. You are firm, steady, and dependable in your allegiance to your husband, not wishy-washy or unpredictable. You joyfully support him long-term. This is what the minister needs, and I think he needs it all the more because of the public nature of his calling. He needs the kind of wife who brings him good, over and over again, day-in and day-out.

This kind of loyalty ought to be an established tone in the marriage and in the home. Everyone should be able to assume it. In this house we are loyal to one another; we trust each other. This is a climate of grace.

Loyalty is rare. People look out for their own interests and they ditch or they flake or they switch sides when they feel like it. Loyalty is a matter of the *heart*. A loyal heart is a steady heart, a heart with a solid commitment. No wavering. You can see it in Psalm 57:7, "My *heart* is steadfast, O God, my *heart* is steadfast; I will sing and give praise." And again in Psalm 112:7, "His heart is steadfast, trusting in the Lord."

Our first obligation as Christian women is to have steadfast hearts to God. All our earthly loyalty is derived from His. He is the author and source of all our loyalty.

Next, the wife must be loyal to her husband. She has promised to be loyal and faithful sexually in thought, word, and deed. This means she is content with her man and not looking for male attention elsewhere. She doesn't flirt or get too comfortable with other men. She keeps a courteous, friendly distance.

When Doug and I were first married, we made some hard-and-fast rules about how we each would interact with the opposite sex. Later when he became a minister, we felt all the more committed to guarding both our marriage and our testimony to those both inside and outside the church. Many churches have been shipwrecked by a pastor who was unwise in his relationships with the women in his congregation. After thirty years in the ministry, we are more convinced than ever that the elders and ministers need to be very careful when it comes to giving pastoral help to needy women.

These hard-and-fast rules helped set the tone for Doug's ministry in the church, and they were just as much a protection for me as they were for him. I never had to worry about whether some needy woman was getting too attached to him. For example, neither of us ever spends one-on-one time with someone of the opposite sex. That means Doug doesn't take one of the ladies out for coffee or meet her for lunch. I don't chum around with any of the men. I don't give a man a ride somewhere, and Doug doesn't give a lady a ride across town

If he needs to meet with a woman for counseling, he has an office with big windows in the double doors, and there are lots of people in the office and in the building. When he is counseling a woman, he does not hold her hand or pat her arm. He keeps his hands to himself. He does not give her a hug when she arrives or when she leaves. He opens the counseling with a brief prayer, but he does not pray with a woman over her situation. If he is in a counseling situation where the woman needs sexual advice, he often hands it off to me, and I begin meeting with her instead. A woman he is counseling does not have his cell phone number unless it is a critical situation where she may need emergency help.

Years ago my daughter received a Christian book on marriage, and one of the hot tips was a mild suggestion that husbands should not travel with their secretaries. I remember my daughter being aghast at the idea that some people had to be told this. A pastor should not have a close relationship with his secretary or *any* woman who is not family. He should be courteous, friendly, and distant to them all. When women are a little intimidated by my husband, I see it as a good sign. I don't want women to feel too chummy with him.

Years ago, a young unmarried woman was meeting with me once a week for a Bible study on an evening when Doug was out. One night when he came home, she mentioned to us that she felt close to me but not to Doug. I remember Doug saying, "Good. You're not supposed to feel close to me." That surprised her, but when we explained it to her, she understood.

A minister should be approachable and warm without being too chummy to the women. My husband does not hug women in the congregation except on rare occasions. One of those exceptions is an elderly widow in our church who gives him a hug each week. And the little kids like to give him hugs. I don't hug the men, unless it is my family. Occasionally I may be on the receiving end of more affection than I want, and this is a delicate situation. I can put my hand out to shake hands, but if that doesn't work, I can keep my distance. If it becomes a real issue, my husband could always address it. But generally we both give sideways "Christian" hugs as a friendly courtesy. I certainly have no issue with such things.

Now you may think that we are too jumpy. But I tell you I have seen some bad behavior and some unwise behavior. I have seen pastors give long, lingering hugs to women in the church all in the name of Christian love. But a wise pastor should know better. Could that woman respond to his physical attention in a way she shouldn't? Could she be stumbled by her pastor? And is the pastor kidding himself about why he is giving her such attention? Is he putting her in a weird situation, invading her space? Maybe she does not know how to tactfully push him (her pastor!) away. And how does it make the pastor's wife feel as she is looking on? What about his children? A good pastor will be aware of the minefield here, and he will see that unwise behavior on his part can be a source of discomfort on many levels for many people.

It seems like I have been writing this for the ministers themselves rather than to their wives. But, no, I believe wives have a big part in this. First you need to discuss these things with your husbands. If you have been struggling with any jealousy because your husband is too close to a woman in your church, you need to speak to him about it. Jealousy is a good thing for a self-respecting wife to feel if her husband is bestowing too much attention on someone else. But jealousy can be a bad thing if is coming from an overly needy, insecure wife who is over-reacting. A pastor needs his wife's support and input, and she can offer valuable insights and feedback. Don't overlook this important area; it will protect your marriage from unnecessary troubles.

A loyal wife goes to her husband first for advice, counsel, and comfort, not to another man or woman. She doesn't pour out her troubles or feelings or needs to someone other than her husband. She doesn't bottle those feelings up either. Her husband hears about them. Loyalty means protecting the relationship. If there are issues they are working through, she does not share it willy-nilly with friends or relatives. A loyal wife cooperates and tries to work things out. If they need help, they decide as a couple to get it.

A wise woman is <u>loyal with her tongue.</u> This is a central way in which she can bring her husband good and not evil all his days. This means being tight-lipped when necessary, careful to keep confidences. <u>A loyal wife has good things to say about her husband, and</u> she doesn't carelessly share his faults, weaknesses, failures, or sins. Some things don't fall into any of these categories necessarily, but would be what we call TMI (too much information). Would he be glad she shared that with the girls? A loyal wife knows when to be quiet. Her husband has confidence that she would not willingly bring him harm in any way. She guards his reputation, she protects his good name, and she knows how crucial this is.

A minister's wife has to be loyal in the tough times. When the church is being attacked from the outside or from the inside, she must stick with her man more than ever. If the pastor has criticism coming at him from several directions, the last thing he needs is more at home. The other thing he doesn't need is a wife who is falling apart, which just adds to his troubles. Am I saying a minister's wife may never disagree with her husband? No, I'm not saying that. But there is a vast difference between a respectful disagreement with a teachable spirit, and blatant criticism and disrespect. She needs to know the difference between giving advice and taking orders.

Finally, some ministers' wives are called to be loyal to their husbands through sin and defeat. If a minister has fallen into some sin that is serious enough to remove him from the ministry, then he needs a loyal wife more than ever. I am not saying that a minister's wife may never divorce her husband when she has biblical grounds. Sadly, sometimes that may be an option. But unless he is the one leaving, she always has the option of sticking with him. She may feel pretty devastated (and with good cause), but her loyalty can help him get things right. In this case, I would hope the minister's wife would have access to wise counsel from the right people.

Sometimes it is a child who has been disloyal to the family by disobedience to God. Again, a loyal wife will be a great asset as the minister leads his family. She needs to follow his leadership as he navigates the difficulty. If he determines that he should step down from the ministry because of the behavior of one of his children, his wife's loyalty and support will be indispensable. These are hard things, but in God's providence, they can be used for great good. A wife's loyalty only increases the opportunities for good to come out of the troubles.

chapter 3

STUMBLING THE

MINISTER

We all want to be five-star helpers for our minister husbands, looking for ways to cheer them on as they preach, teach, and fulfill their various duties, but we can sometimes be the means of stumbling our husbands rather than helping them.

This is not a new concept. Our mother Eve is our primary example of the helper gone amiss, so we know we are fully capable of following in her footsteps and "handing our husbands the apple," so to speak. *Here, honey. Have a bite of this!* O Lord, deliver us from being the means by which our husbands fall.

But how does this happen? The obvious temptations are clear; it's the subtle ones that can trip us up. The obvious stumbling-block wife is the one we have all seen or heard about who rules the roost and pins back her husband's ears with her insistence that he do things her way. We have a name for this kind of woman. She is the battle axe, and look out if you come within striking distance. She demands attention, standing there with her arms crossed and her foot tapping. Though your temptation to rule over your husband may be more subtle than this, it is just as deadly.

Consider this possibility. We want our husbands to preach the Word boldly, but what if his bold preaching ruffles some feathers, as it most assuredly will? A minister's wife must be on guard against the temptation to get her husband to tone it down. "But if he keeps preaching like that, everyone is going to leave the church." Of course it all depends on what "preaching like that" means. Proverbs 28:1 says, "But the righteous are bold as a lion." What is "great boldness in the faith" (1 Tim. 3:13) unless it is preaching without fear? And what's to be afraid of? If there were no hard consequences to preaching, then there would be no need for boldness. Boldness is required where there is *danger*.

I think that most women by nature prefer to get along. I confess that I number myself among them, preferring approval to disapproval. Who wouldn't? Don't we all want our husbands to be appreciated rather than criticized, well received rather than dismissed, marginalized, or overlooked? Most wives like it even less when their husbands encounter real hostility either from the congregation, the larger Christian community, or from the unbelieving world. This is only natural and understandable, but it is also a snare. A wife can think she is helping her husband to be more rhetorically effective when she is encouraging him to tone it down, but in reality she may be motivated to keep everyone happy. Having everyone pleased with our husbands is not the highest good. It never is. And once a man begins to preach and teach and lead a church to gain approval from his wife or his congregation rather than from God, he and his church and his ministry are all doomed (and his marriage is probably doomed as well).

We have all heard stories of bold ministers who laid down their lives for the Gospel. This is all well and good when we read about it at a safe distance of two hundred years or several thousand miles. But what if it is our husbands whose lives are endangered? At such times, not only do ministers need prayer for boldness, but so do we wives. Even the Apostle Paul asked for prayer "that in it I may speak boldly, as I ought to speak" (Eph. 6:19–20). And if *he* needed prayer for boldness, knowing what was at stake, so do our husbands, and so do we. I especially appreciate the last five words in the verse above: *as I ought to speak.* The Christian minister has a duty to speak faithfully, and he needs prayer for boldness to do it.

Not only are ministers' wives tempted to urge their husbands to soften the message to stay out of trouble, but we may also be tempted in many small ways to urge our husbands to back away from speaking the Word too powerfully and boldly in the public square. It may be safe to say those things within the walls of the church on a Sunday morning, but in the newspaper? On the radio? On the internet? That kind of boldness may cause him to lose friends or his standing (as Mr. Nice Guy) in the broader Christian community. He may lose opportunities for advancement. He may not be invited back to speak. Some of the prominent or wealthy supporters may withdraw their (much-needed) financial gifts. Some of your own friends may be offended and pull away. These are the circumstances when the minister's wife is called to be courageous. <u>If he is being faithful, he needs a faithful helper who won't shrink back when everyone else does.</u>

We live in a day when the church has become compromised over many issues. It takes a courageous minister to renounce women's ordination, sodomy, abortion, infanticide, euthanasia. Many ministers would prefer to keep preaching on "safe" topics and dance around the edges when asked direct questions about direct texts. It is possible that many do so at the urging of their wives. What a terrible situation for a minister to be caught in: if he addresses the hard issues, he will have an unhappy home. If he draws back, he'll have an unhappy conscience but a "peaceful" home life. What the minister really needs to do at such a time is to bring his wife up to speed. He must lead and teach her through the difficulty so that she is prepared to be on the same page. The only other alternative is for the minister to choose to be faithful to his calling while leaving his wife to sort out her own troubles. But that is just cowardice at another level.

So how can we have courage when we know our husbands are going to "catch it" for not shrinking back? We must start in the little (seemingly insignificant) things. Maybe it's as simple as not letting that woman in the congregation who wants more potlucks push you around so that you'll put pressure on your husband. It may include deferring to his judgment to say "no" to that couple who wants to pay your way for a vacation or buy you a new car (and you dread the consequences of turning them down). These are baby steps, but they are good ones. And the more we learn to be God-pleasers and not man-pleasers, the more we will grow in boldness and courage.

This requires *thinking* like Christians. This is God's church, and your husband is His minister. He answers to God Almighty, just like you do. You want your husband to live and preach in a manner worthy of the calling he has received. Remind yourself that if he has received such a calling, then you have been ordained to come along side, standing with him and helping him, encouraging him and comforting him, not giving way to fear.

"Let your conduct be without covetousness; be content with such things as you have. For He Himself has said, "I will never leave you nor forsake you." So we may boldly say: "The Lord is my helper; I will not fear: What can man do to me?" (Heb. 13:5–6).

As we grow to be courageous, faithful women, we will be able to interpret all of the Lord's ways toward us in a positive light. And this will be of great use to us when we are handling the trials that come in the ministry.

chapter 4

FLYING SOLO

As the years roll by, your life will change and so will some of your responsibilities. We must be flexible women, adjusting to these changes by faith. For example, my kids are grown with families of their own now. At the worship service, they sit together with their children and not with me, which is as it should be. I am accustomed to flying solo at church as well as at other events.

For example, at most of the weddings I attend (and we have quite a number), I sit without my husband. That's normal. And after the wedding, he is sometimes hard to find, but eventually we connect and make our way to the reception, where he may have to disappear again. This is what we do, and I know the dance steps fairly well by now.

The same goes for worship. It is a rare Sunday when I am seated with my husband all through the service. But I don't mind. I have the privilege of having him be my minister as well as my husband. When the kids were little, I sometimes wished for another pair of hands, but the kids were great. They never pulled any terrible stunts during worship. And, back in those days, we had a children's church service for them during the sermon, so it really wasn't oh-so-very tough. But there were still times that I felt rather stranded. I've learned a lot about navigating since then!

Not only is he gone during the worship service, but he is busy for an hour or more afterwards, visiting people at the door. I try to connect to people and enjoy the time for fellowship. When the kids were young and hungry and eager to get home to lunch, they had to learn to wait. They fellowshipped too, and it didn't hurt any of us.

As the crowd thins after church, I try to keep an eye on my husband, and I can usually tell when he's ready to go. Then I make my appearance, and if I've read him right, we head out the door.

When the kids were little, of course I had to miss church when one or more was sick. Recently another minister's wife asked me what I did to make it a special day for the kids when they had to miss church. I'm afraid I don't remember! I hope I read some Bible stories to them. I always tried to make sick times as sweet as possible, but I really don't recall what I did on those Sundays. You would think I would at least remember what I did for the six weeks when the chicken pox went through the house, but I don't. The only thing I remember about that was the college student who asked me where I went to church! I thought he was joking, but he seriously thought maybe I attended church elsewhere!

When we travel to visit a congregation where my husband is speaking, of course I find myself solo quite a bit, depending on where we are. One of the things that can help me navigate that kind of event is to think of myself as a hostess. I know that may sound strange, especially if we are the guests, but here's what I mean.

If you are visiting a church where your husband is preaching, be friendly and outgoing. Your husband may be whisked off to pray with the elders before church, and you may feel stranded. Don't worry about it. Relax. Be approachable, but if everyone is busy, just go sit down and check your email (assuming you have that kind of phone) or read over the bulletin. If you have a posse of children with you, you've brought your own companions and entertainment. Find them a place to settle in and don't feel at sea waiting to be "escorted" some place. Hostess yourself. Show yourself around. Don't be afraid to introduce yourself and get into conversations. Be a participant and not a spectator.

Of course there are exceptions to this policy. For example, if your husband is conducting a graveside service, and you don't know anyone involved, keep a respectful distance and don't try to intrude. You are there for your husband, not for the family whom you do not know. Your husband appreciates your presence. You have a role to play. Just take your opportunities as you get them, but don't feel left out. If you feel left out, you will feel uncomfortable or hurt, and there is really no need to. It can't be helped. It's part of the job.

I have visited places where I was kindly escorted everywhere and looked after, and I have visited places where I had to fend for myself. Both are fine, but it's much better for me if I assume the latter will be the case. Then I am pleasantly surprised if it is otherwise, and no offense is taken if I am left to myself. I'm afraid I had to learn this the hard way by being in awkward circumstances, but now I'm more relaxed about it. There's no sin (that I know of) in feeling at loose ends. We just need to get good at navigating those moments.

Flying solo can also be the case when your husband is called away for meetings, or counseling, or even when he is in his office preparing for Sunday morning worship. This is no surprise. This is his calling. So we wives need to be the kind of women who can manage on our own. We can view it as part of our contribution to his ministry. In other words, we can carry our own weight and then some.

I am not suggesting that the minister's wife is left all alone in the world to tough it out. But there will be times. We need to be prepared to hostess ourselves through those times and not think something weird has happened. If we are cheerful and prepared, that's half the battle. Believe it or not, you may seem very self-confident to everyone else. In fact, as funny as it may sound to you, you may even seem intimidating to some. They may feel more uncomfortable than you do. So go the extra distance and reach out to the stranger. Assume responsibility. You will enjoy it more, and so will everyone else.

chapter 5

PRAYING FOR THE

PASTOR

Your husband needs prayer, and you must determine to surround him with prayer every day. Of course all wives should pray for their husbands, but the Scripture gives some specific guidelines on how to pray for the minister. Being a minister is a challenge that requires much faith, and the minister's wife, if she is paying attention, has a close-up view of some of the great demands placed upon the minister. And when we are praying for our husbands, we may notice how often we have a hand in helping him as we see God answer our prayers.

So what should the content of our prayers be for our husbands as they assume their duties throughout the week, and particularly as they minister the Word on the Lord's Day? I have gathered a few suggestions from 1 and 2 Timothy. It's not an exhaustive list, but this should get us started.

1. "May the Lord give you understanding in all things" (1 Tim. 2:2).

Pray that he will grow in his understanding of the Word so that he can apply it to the myriad things that come up in the congregation. Some of these issues and tangles require tremendous wisdom to sort out. So pray that the Lord will give him ongoing understanding and wisdom "in all things."

2. "Preach the Word! Be ready in season and out of season. Convince, rebuke, exhort, with all longsuffering and teaching" (2 Tim. 4:2).

Whew! This is quite a tall order. Pray that your husband will preach the Word faithfully with long-term patience. Since my husband has been pastoring our church for such a long time now, I can see the need for patience. A whole new generation has grown up in our church, and they are now raising their own kids. This means my husband has to go over the same basic things one more time. And again. Some in the congregation were little kids back when he did that series. And of course there are many new members. So pray that your husband will be always ready for whatever the situation calls for, whether it is to convince, rebuke, exhort, or teach. And this takes us back to #1.

3. "Guard what was committed to your trust" (1 Tim. 6:20). "Hold fast the pattern of sound words . . . in faith and love which are in Christ Jesus" (1 Tim. 1:13).

Your husband has been entrusted with nothing less than the gospel. He may feel overwhelmed with the greatness of the task and daunted by his own limitations. Most great preachers feel this way. He must guard his calling and not abandon it. You must help him do this, not only by praying for him, but also by not growing weary yourself. How many wives have been the means of drawing their husbands away from their calling because of the difficulties that attend it? By respecting his calling and praying for his loyalty and faithfulness to it, you will be equipped to help him in this.

4. "For God has not given us a spirit of fear, but of power and of love and of a sound mind" (2 Tim. 1:7).

Pray that your husband will be empowered by the Holy Spirit, preaching with authority and power. Pray that he will be as bold as a lion, never shrinking back from preaching the whole truth because of any fear of public opinion or of upsetting certain people (including you). And pray that you will share in the same boldness and not shrink away from him when he is faithful and fearless.

5. "Be strong in the grace that is in Christ Jesus" (1 Tim. 2:1).

Pray for great grace to rest upon your husband. Grace is the source of his strength.

6. "Endure hardship as a good soldier of Jesus Christ" (2 Tim. 2:3).

Pray that your husband will not be surprised at any hardship that accompanies his calling, and pray that he will endure it cheerfully. Soldiers don't have an easy life. Wives are co-soldiers with their husbands. Share the hardships with him, with gratitude and not discontent. Pray for ways to lighten his load and use the home front to comfort him. Remember who it is you serve. Wives can be the source of discouragement to their husbands when they become unhappy with the hardships. Pray that you will have the endurance of a good soldier yourself.

7. "Be gentle to all, able to teach, patient, in humility correcting those who are in opposition" (2 Tim. 2:24–25).

Pray that your husband will exhibit all the fruit of the Spirit. Some in the congregation may test his patience! Pray for him to be humble and gentle and patient in all things. And how can you pray this for him without praying for yourself the same way? Don't be offended when some oppose your husband. Apparently Paul thought it would be a common enough occurrence to include directions to Timothy about it.

8. "Be watchful in all things, endure afflictions, do the work of an evangelist, fulfill your ministry" (2 Tim. 4:5).

Pray that he will be watchful, alert, and on his guard. You don't want your husband to be blindsided by anything, so pray that he will see things coming and anticipate possible problems while there is still time to prevent them. Pray that he can and will fulfill his ministry (which goes back to #3). Pray that he won't be a quitter but will hunker down and endure the hard times. That means that you must be the kind of woman who will cheer him on, and not be the kind of woman who wants him to throw in the towel. Fulfilling his ministry means finishing what he started, performing his duties, and not giving up.

9. "Let the elders who rule well be counted worthy of double honor, especially those who labor in the word and doctrine" (1 Tim. 5:17).

Pray that your husband (and all the elders) will be good, gracious, merciful, and wise rulers of the congregation. And notice the use of the word *labor*. It is hard work to teach and preach. Pray that he will work hard, and don't think of your husband's calling as a nine-to-five job. In addition, if your husband is preaching the Word, treat him with double honor.

10. "Do not lay hands on anyone hastily, nor share in other people's sins; keep yourself pure" (1 Tim. 5:22).

Finally, pray that your husband will be uncontaminated by the world, and then help him by being the kind of wife he can confide in, trust in, and be more than satisfied by. In all these things, as we pray for our husbands, we reap the benefits. We grow in our appreciation of what they are doing; we become more aware of the significant role we have as their helpers; and we find that as we pray for them, we look for God to do the same for us, and so we become more like Christ as we pray for our husbands to be more like Christ. And this is good.

PART 2

Your Children

chapter 6

THE CONGREGATION
AT HOME

I believe that my husband would agree with me that some of his very best parishioners are our children. My husband began ministering in our church when our children were very young, and they have accompanied us on this journey. And since they have grown up in the minister's home, they know the background story very well. They have been our loyal companions, sharing our concerns, offering ideas, and giving their input. They have a true interest in the health of the congregation, and they care very much about their father's ministry. This has been a very central blessing to us. It is hard to estimate the impact their love and loyalty have had on us, and how that has both equipped and enabled us to do what God has called us to do. For me, they have been a steady source of comfort, help, and peace; for my minister husband, they have been a strong support and joy.

A minister's family needs to be a team that enjoys being together. Our children have always been an immense pleasure to us. Now that they are adults with families of their own, they continue to stimulate us, delight and refresh us, help us, and sharpen us. We would be seriously handicapped without them.

Now you may be a young minister's wife with two little kids and another one on the way. You may wonder how you are supposed to meet all the needs in the congregation when you are so busy meeting the needs of these little people. Let me give you a suggestion: don't try! You are not called to meet the needs of the congregation; you are actually called to meet the needs of the minister and his kids. You are his helper, and there is no one who can help him like you. He needs some clean socks and a fresh shirt. He needs a hot meal at the end of a long day. He needs a loving and cheerful wife. He needs kids who are glad to see him. So keep your eye on your true mission. Your congregation will be much more blessed in the long run if you take good care of their minister.

We made some commitments when our kids were very little. My husband determined that he did not want them to grow up seeing the back of his head as he went out the door, so he kept his evening obligations to a minimum, and he only traveled occasionally. He never made the family feel like they were not as important as his "real" calling as a minister. Far from it. Saturdays were the day he took the kids out for donuts or to the library or to their favorite stomping grounds on the mountain. He coached our daughter's softball team, started the lacrosse club for our son, and drove us all around the countryside to be at the basketball or football games. He helped start their Christian school and taught all kinds of classes there to help get it off the ground. He was (and is) a big part of their lives.

At dinner time the kids could ask him questions and tell him the stories of the day. He would listen and laugh and give them advice and input. They never saw church as a competition for his time. He was always home for dinner at 5:30, with rare exception, and he still is. While they were growing up, he never shut himself off in an office at the other end of the house but would read in the living room, and he would put his book down any time they (or I) wanted to talk.

I cannot tell you how grateful for this I am. At the time, of course, I knew it was good that we were pouring ourselves into our children. But now, from this vantage point, I see the fruit with my own eyes. Our kids are still the best company. They are unflinchingly loyal and full of pastoral insights of their own. We could not have weathered some of the trials and controversies without them! "Happy is the man that hath his quiver full of them: they shall not be ashamed, but they shall speak with the enemies in the gate" (Ps. 127:5).

So don't muddle your priorities. Don't be distracted by "ministry" opportunities in the church. Of course we should extend ourselves to the families in the church, but not at the expense of our kids. Now I'm not saying the kids should rule the roost. Of course not. But if the kids are not doing well, then the family's not doing well, and then the minister is not really qualified to be leading others. This is an important point that many ministers have neglected. They may be so over-committed at the church that their family sees little of them. And then as the family starts to show the tell-tale signs of neglect, the minister feels overwhelmed by all the needs at home, so he may pour himself into the church all the more where he can feel successful. But this just makes everything worse at home, and the vicious cycle gains momentum. That's when you hear ministers explaining away some of the scriptural qualifications for leadership in the home.

Some of you may feel like your husband is always heading out the door, so this chapter may hit you rather hard. I don't want you to feel discouraged! Pray first. Maybe you are just in one of those "hunker down" times, and this is not the way your home is normally.

But what if it is normal? What if he is gone so much that the kids do see the back of his head more than they should? In that case, please go to your husband prayerfully and respectfully. Ask him to consider how much he is gone away from home. Don't be accusative, but lay out your concerns to him and ask him to pray about it. Don't ask him to make a quick decision. He may feel trapped and stuck. Pray with and for him in this, and then be patient. Trust God to provide a way for him to get help. I once wrote our elders (with my husband's permission) asking them to please find him an assistant. This may be what you need to do as well. But it's very important that you not get into an adversarial relationship with your husband over this. You are on his team, and you want him to be effective in his calling as both father and pastor. You want him to feel like you are cheering for him, not booing against him. If he thinks you are just criticizing, that will only make things worse.

Wives are helpers. If you want to help him see how things are going at home, you have to make sure you are really seeing them clearly yourself. If you are bogged down with hurt feelings or resentment, you will not be in a position to help him. Clear your own heart and mind first. Then bring your concerns to him, and ask God to bless you both with wisdom and grace.

chapter 7

QUALIFICATIONS

Paul says to Timothy that a bishop or overseer must "rule his own house well, having his children in submission with all reverence (for if a man does not know how to rule his own house, how will he take care of the church of God?)" (1 Tim. 3:4–5). And Paul repeats this qualification for elders in Titus 1:6: "having faithful children not accused of dissipation or insubordination."

Today this qualification is often explained away, ignored, or re-interpreted for obvious reasons: it seems too hard. Who can be a minister if the children have to meet this standard? But a faithful minister is one who takes God's Word very seriously, and so this qualification is a sobering one. Who is sufficient for these things?

It would be far better for a minister to take a leave of absence from his pastoral duties and get the family squared away, than to let things continue to deteriorate at home. The pulpits of God's churches need faithful men in them, men who do not take His Word lightly. And they need wives who do not take this lightly either. Wives can do a lot to keep their homes and children in order, and this is a central way they can be of tremendous help to their husbands. But they also need to keep their minister husbands briefed on the morale of the troops. If a wife is just putting on a poker face and pushing through, thinking she should not burden her husband with the troubles at home, she is being unwise. It will probably be just a matter of time before she craters. Don't let that happen. A pastor's first calling is to shepherd his home. And if his home is shepherded well, it is a good indicator that the church will be also.

One of the things my husband learned from his father was that this qualification was to be taken at face value. If a minister's home is not in order, then he is simply not qualified to be a minister. When my husband became a minister, we were committed to this principle. We believed that Doug's first calling was to be a faithful husband and father, and his ministry to the saints was secondary. There are two ways to take this qualification: one way is to put a heavy load on the children; the other way (and I believe the proper way) is to put a load on the parents. Parents know that Jesus loves to carry our burdens. He loves to bless us when we seek to walk by faith, when we try with all our might to please Him in how we live, and how we bring up our children before Him.

chapter 8

FIRST PRINCIPLES

Now that so many years have passed, I confess that I have forgotten many *details* of our lives with our children when they were very small, but I do remember the *principles* that guided us. For example, we taught our children from the time they were very small that they were not going to date (they didn't), that they were going to marry like-minded Christians (they did), that they were not going to the government schools where they would be taught by unbelievers (or by believers who would not be free to teach as Christians), and that *they were the most important thing their father was doing.*

After they began attending the Christian school that Doug helped to start (and when I say *helped*, I mean he literally poured himself out), I can remember having this conversation from time to time at the dinner table. If one of the students was expelled for serious misbehavior, one of our children would invariably ask at the dinner table, "Dad, if one of us had done that, would you step down from the ministry?" And Doug would say without hesitation, "Yes, I would have already submitted my resignation. If you were doing things like that, it would be clear that I was not being a very good dad, so I would need to stop being a minister and just focus on being a better dad."

Our children did not feel threatened by this. Rather, they saw that their father was very serious about his commitment *to them*, to raise them in a way that honored the Lord. They knew that they were his best qualification, and they took their duty very seriously to honor his commitment. Understanding that he was loyal to them made them very loyal to him, and they still are. He loved them, was committed to them, and took his duty to rear them before the Lord very seriously. So rather than making them feel the pressure to be good, this understanding made them humble and loyal. This was so much the case, that if an elder's child misbehaved to the extent that the elder had to step down, it infuriated our children that any child could take their father's calling so lightly.

I want you to understand that this commitment to having our household in order put pressure on us, not on our children. They felt loved, not pressured. They felt secure knowing that they outranked all those other people in the church that their father loved and served, and that this was the way it should be.

Now having said all this, I want to make it clear that our children were sinners just like all the other children in the congregation. But they were never rebellious, and I have to say, they never shamed us or embarrassed us in any way. They knew that if they were rebellious, their father would resign from the ministry and give himself to them more diligently. He said many times that he would rather take a job flipping burgers at McDonald's than be a hypocrite, telling other people how to love their children and train them up to love and fear God, if his own children were not doing well.

The minister's family is a real family, not a fake family. They should feel a good and godly pressure to live in an upright manner, but this does not mean that the minister's family is holier than the rest of the congregation. But it does mean that the minister's family cannot cut corners. Our children felt a good pressure to live in a manner that was consistent with their father's calling, and this really was a good pressure, not a bad pressure. They saw firsthand many times what happened to people who decided to forsake the Lord and do things their own way. This show-and-tell in the real world was a rich blessing for our children. They saw how important it was to live for Christ in the big things and the small things. They heard and saw their father being patient with all kinds of people in all kinds of circumstances at all kinds of times, day and night. And it was good for them.

One of the results of this upbringing has been that each of our children has a keen pastoral instinct. Each has a pastoral radar that is seldom wrong. From time to time one of them will mention something to their father like, "Dad, just thought you should know that so-in-so is clearly not doing well." And it's uncanny how often they are right.

With sixteen grandchildren in the weekly worship service, I have grown accustomed to seeing my son or one of my sons-in-law leave the worship service to deal with a little one who needs correction. I am thankful when I see it for two reasons: because it is a sign of good parenting, and because I'm glad the congregation can see our grandchildren are just like all the other little people who need love and faithful discipline and correction.

I think many pastors' wives feel pressure to have a *perfect* family. But that is not the goal. We are to strive to have a *faithful* family. Some ministers may have the same standard, but the pressure is on the kids rather than on the parents where it belongs. Paul's qualification is not given to the kids; it is directed to the elder or overseer or bishop.

Pastors' children should not have to share their dad with everyone else. They should be able to enjoy their father and their status as his children. They should not be made to feel like second-rate citizens because everyone else sees more of their dad than they do. This will only embitter them toward their parents, and, by extension, it will embitter them against the Lord.

My husband learned this from his own father. Once when Doug was pretty little, his dad was counseling someone in the living room of their home. Doug kept running in to ask his dad a question or show him something, and the man getting the counsel was starting to get annoyed at the interruptions. Finally he said, "Can't you make your son quit interrupting us?" Jim laughed and explained, "But he's more important than you are! He's my son. He can come in as often as he wants." That is one of the reasons why my husband grew up knowing exactly who he was and where he stood with his father. And that is why he didn't want to short-change our own kids.

So how does the minister's wife help with this? In many, many ways. Our duty is to help keep our husband posted on how all the children are doing, to give him a heads up when one of them needs more time (we called it a low tank). We should not have unrealistic standards for the kids, thinking that if the three-year-old throws a fit, our husband is disqualified. The standard is faithfulness over the long haul, not obedience or disobedience at any given moment.

I'd like to add an important note to this. Although my husband would have resigned from the ministry if one of our children had rebelled, we would not pressure other ministers to do the same. In other words, if a fellow minister had six disobedient children, my husband might consider calling into question his qualification for ministry. But if he had five faithful children, and one straying, my husband would be reluctant to call him on the carpet. What we expected of ourselves was not the same thing we would enforce on others. So, I am certainly not suggesting that ministers' wives start policing the other families of church officers. This is about *us* and *our children*. We want to be faithful ourselves, and that is plenty to keep us occupied.

Some pastors' wives can feel apologetic or embarrassed if their own family is healthy and happy and prospering while many in the congregation are up against it. Don't give way to guilt over this. That only robs God of the gratitude He should be receiving from us for blessing us so richly. When women with problems tell you that you just don't understand because your family is doing well, don't get defensive or apologetic. Agree with them. Of course you don't understand. How could we? But Jesus does. Our duty is to point them to Him.

PART 3

Church Duties

chapter 9

THE NEW PASTOR'S
WIFE

Some of you may be married to a minister fresh out of seminary. You may be settling into your husband's first church where he is working as the minister or assistant minister, and most likely you are getting situated in your new role as a minister's wife. So this section is especially for you (although I hope those of you who have been married to a minister for many years will find some encouragement here as well).

If your husband is a new pastor, he can't exactly tell you what to expect. You may not know your congregation very well yet, and it will take time to settle in. So the first thing I would say to you is *take it slowly*. Don't rush things. Otherwise, you might start something you can't finish.

Perhaps you are thinking great thoughts about what a glamorous thing it is to be in the ministry. Maybe you are thinking you will host a Bible study in your home twice a week and a prayer meeting one morning a week and have folks to dinner every Friday, and set aside one night as an evangelistic outreach to your neighborhood. These are all very good things in themselves, but please, please do not do this! You will burn yourself and your husband out in six months (or less) and your church will wonder what happened.

Ease in slowly. Start in the shallow end of the pool. It would be far, far better to have guests for a meal once a week and stick with that for a few months. Then after your husband has gotten to know the needs of the congregation, he may want to start a Bible study in your home. Be sure that you are not such an enthusiastic cheerleader that your husband is tempted to over-commit your family. Then when you collapse under the weight of all you have taken on, he will wonder what happened to your pom-poms. Take your time. There is no fire! Don't be too eager to push him out the door to "minister" to others.

Something else to note here: this is your husband's calling and ministry, not yours. Of course you are co-laborers in Christ. But it's very important to defer to him and not try to lead the way. Does he really want you inviting the neighbors over for dinner? Was it his idea? Now, if he is all for it, then press on. But he may have other concerns or other people he feels burdened to minister to. Find out who they are and make your hospitality an outworking of his ministry, and then it will become yours too.

As I have said before, your ministry is your husband. So as you try to find your place in helping him to minister to others, defer to him. What does he want you doing? Does he want you to stay busy at home and keep the kids happy? Then do it, remembering that God is going to lead you through your husband. This might be contrary to your idea of the incredible, indispensable minister's super-wife that you envisioned. Actually, you are indispensable in your home, to your children and to your husband. Don't forget this! And remember that you want to defer to his style of ministry, his preferences and his guidance.

If you are just starting a family or don't have children yet, you may have more flexibility. Even so, take it slowly and follow your husband's wisdom and leading. He will be adjusting to his calling, taking on new responsibilities, and this is no easy thing. It is exhausting work to teach, preach, study, counsel, and prepare, and even though he may love what he is doing, he is still going to need to rest. He may long for you to keep his home life simple and comfortable, not full of guests and ministry each night when he comes home. So work to keep the house a pleasant place to come home to. That is by far the most important work you do, and the best thing you can give your congregation is a minister who is content. If you have a house full of children, that is all the more reason to keep your home life as uncomplicated as possible. The children need to be with him, and your evenings ought to be free so that he can read to them and play with them and catch up with you.

When women in the church call you and ask you to lead a Bible study or organize a luncheon or host something at your house, just thank them and tell them you will talk to your husband and get back to them. If it is a good idea, and your husband thinks it's a good idea, and there are no hindrances, then by all means go for it. But you don't want to put pressure on your husband to let you do it because you are feeling pressure from the church ladies and you don't want to let them down. Keep the lines of authority clear. He may know how frazzled you will be if you take this on. Don't be afraid to say no, even if they tell you all the other ministers' wives before you did such-and-such. Conversely, if your husband really wants you to host a ladies' luncheon, and you are too timid, then trust the Lord, submit to your husband, and do it. God will bless your obedience even if the whole thing bombs. At least then your husband will see you are not suited to that role. My point here is to follow his lead. He's your pastor too!

Now some of you have the gifts and abilities to actually pull off the kind of life I described above, with Bible studies every night and guests non-stop. So I bless you! Way to go! But that is not the way my husband and I are made. We would have completely collapsed. God will enable you to do what He is calling you to do with the gifts He has given you. Just because we could not manage that, doesn't mean no one can.

Over the years that my husband has ministered here, our church has changed its name twice, adjusted its theology, met in multiple places, seen many people come and go, and grown in numbers. But our family has stayed pretty much the same through it all. Of course we have grown with the church: our kids have moved out, gotten married, and have families of their own. But our home life has always been centered around my husband. The kids couldn't wait to see him, and dinner was always a time to talk over the day and ask him questions. He read to them for hundreds of hours. Was there ever an emergency counseling situation that took him away? Yes. Phone calls? Yes. But he tried to keep as much of it as he could at the office. Home was where he could get out his guitar and sing with and for the kids, and now it's for the grandkids.

Our church has never had dozens of programs and meetings because it would have killed us and everyone else. We are all busy with our families. When our kids were in junior high and high school, we had Bible studies for their age group in our home. When they were in college, we had college gatherings here. I believe that our commitment to our home life has not only blessed our family, but it has blessed our whole congregation. They know that their pastor views his responsibility as a husband and father very seriously, and they have seen him live that out before them. When we keep first things first, God blesses our lives with peace and contentment. So as you settle into your calling as a minister's wife, remember that your husband is just flesh and blood like you. He needs food and rest, refreshment and companionship, love and peace. Your congregation will be more likely to prosper under his leadership if you are seeing to it that he is cared for.

I wonder how those unmarried men in the ministry can do it. They go home each night to a dark house or apartment where no one has fixed them supper or put a flower on the table or washed and sorted their socks. It would be a lonely and difficult life. So make the most of your opportunities, be a faithful and hard-working wife, and God will open doors if He wants you to be involved in more ministry in your church.

chapter 10

YOUR RELATIONSHIP TO

THE CHURCH

As I have mentioned before, we must remember who we are. We are wives, not elders or pastors. I remember when I felt responsible for the congregation as though I was the church hostess. That is a job way out of my depth! What a relief it was when I discovered I was not in charge of keeping everyone happy. If something went wrong in the service, I could sit like the rest of the congregation and see what would happen. I didn't have to solve any problems (or worry over who would). These responsibilities were delegated to capable men who could handle them. I discovered that I was one of the sheep, not a shepherd. Women love to fill a void, but there are times when we absolutely must not.

As a member of the congregation, I have responsibilities just like everyone else. However, I believe the pastor's wife has an extra duty of being a good example in this area. Not for show, but for real. She ought to be the kind of church member who is a delight to lead. To do that, she needs to have her head in the game.

A pastor's wife (and the children) should be easy to lead. Proverbs 10:8 says that the wise in heart will *receive commands*. That means no squawking about decisions the church leadership makes. It means no eye-rolling at the music selections. She should be the kind of person who makes shepherding the flock a joy and not a burden. This means that the minister's wife follows her husband and the decisions that the elder board (or whatever governing body your church has) makes with a quiet spirit. If they change the time of the worship service, she should cheerfully adjust her schedule. If they change the name of the church, she should not complain about it. She should always assume the best and thank God for the leaders in the church who lead the flock.

Someone said that a teachable spirit is the best proof of a wise heart. A humble heart receives and welcomes teaching. We ought to be serious students, listening diligently to the preached Word. And if we are busy with little ones, we may have to listen to the sermon recording later. In other words, we should do what we can to participate as much as we can in the worship service.

We should think about how we dress for church and how the children behave, not because we are ministers' wives, but because we want to please the Lord. Consider whether you are punctual, prepared, and attentive. Do you sing robustly, follow the liturgy, participate fully, and follow the sermon carefully? Are the kids learning to do the same?

Our children must be reverent, but I don't mean pietistic. We want pious children, but not pietistic children. True piety is a good thing. Pietism is external religion for show-boaters. We want our children to have a high regard for God's worship, but they will only do this if we show them how. Yes, we want them to be in good order, but we want them to be internalizing the standards, not simply complying externally.

Now this is all easy for *me* to say. My children are all grown and I now sit through the service in the front row without them. They sit in various parts of the building with their own batches of children. I recognize the voices of my grandchildren from time to time, and I see my children carrying one or the other out of the service and back in again. So, it's easy for me to say all this to you who have a bunch of little kids to navigate through the worship service each week!

But I hope I can still be encouraging to you. You are to be a model parishioner because you love your husband and you love his calling and you want to smooth his path as best you can. Not all wives have the privilege of participating as closely in their husbands' calling as the minister's wife does. The doctor's wife is not watching him deliver babies, and the attorney's wife is seldom in the courtroom. The farmer's wife is not out in the field, and the engineer's wife is not doing whatever it is those guys do. The minister's wife has a unique opportunity. She can sit under his teaching with the rest of the congregation, she can participate in many of the church activities that he is involved with. Certainly there are exceptions. She does not sit in on the elders' meetings or counseling appointments or sit beside him while he studies and prepares. But she is able to get a close look at all that he does because his central duties of preaching and teaching are those that she benefits from like everyone else.

Proverbs 10:17 says that he who keeps instruction is in the way of life, but he who refuses correction goes astray. So we ought to value discipline and pay attention to every lesson. Our children will learn from us. We are students with them in Christ's school. When we are convicted in a sermon, we should rejoice and be eager to apply what we have learned.

A good church member gives feedback without biting criticism. Express your gratitude to your husband for his ministry to you and the children. Ask him questions. When others tell you what a great sermon it was, acknowledge what a blessing it was to you as well. Some pastors' wives can feel awkward receiving compliments on behalf of their husbands. But I think we should express our agreement as part of the congregation. We wives are beneficiaries of our husbands' ministry. In fact, I think I must get a double portion because I sit so close to the minster!

We should be good students, not critics. I do not grade my husband's sermon any more than he grades my cooking. I am nourished by his teaching, fed by the Word. I do not grade it with a red pen. Nevertheless, I am praying for him before and during the sermon, trusting that God will use it for great good and His glory.

A good parishioner will keep a lively sense of humor. After all, people are funny, and every church has plenty of people in it. So we must not get weighed down by the funny things people say or do. We don't need to call an elders' meeting because of something someone said. Maybe it was a rude comment. Well then, don't return rudeness for rudeness. Let it go. God sees it. Don't make trouble. If you think it's something serious, hand it off to your husband and see what he thinks.

When it comes to relationships in the church, beware flatterers. Don't let people buy your affection with flattery (or gifts). Don't allow yourself to get into an awkward relationship with someone who gives you gifts with strings (visible or invisible) attached. Sometimes you must say no. This requires wisdom. For example, if someone is clustering around, wanting to give you too much attention in exchange for your friendship, I advise you to keep a cheerful and warm distance. Don't become dependent. Keep your guard up, but don't isolate yourself. You can be friendly and still be careful.

When it comes to the minister's salary, it's best not to know who the big tithers in the church are. Don't adopt a needy persona because you think that is what a minister should be. Some ministers have very small incomes and some have large incomes. Be a good example of tithing and giving without letting your left hand know what your right hand is doing. At the same time, don't apologize for God's blessings when He prospers you. I remember being embarrassed and worried when Doug bought me a microwave back in the early 80's when they were a hot new item. What would the church think of us whooping it up like that? It was worse when a friend joked about the pastor's wife owning a microwave! But we cannot nor should we have to give an account to the congregation when God blesses us. In all this, we must trust the Lord for our finances.

A minister's family should show regular hospitality, but not because they are under some kind of heavy obligation or compulsion. Hospitality should be a "get to" and not a "have to." At the same time, hospitality really is a "have to" for the pastor's family. It is not optional or something to get around to some day. So if you are tempted to be lazy about this, get going! If you are timid about hospitality, you must overcome these fears and open your door! You will learn as you go. Make hospitality something the children enjoy and not something they resent because they are pushed aside. Include them in it. Pray that God will give you a hospitable spirit. Use your home to bless others. Find some never-fail recipes and start feeding people. You will be greatly blessed as you extend yourself this way.

Let me give you a recent, real-life example (and I bet you have a few of your own). I was in the midst of some heavy hospitality back-to-back, two days in a row. I woke up on day two thinking that I was probably going to die. I decided that crying wasn't going to help, so I thanked God and prayed for wisdom and help. He loves to answer prayers like this. And I asked my husband to pray for me as well (which always helps). I prayed for a brilliant idea for a simple menu, got the inspiration, managed to pull it off (by the grace of God), and was truly blessed in the process. We are not super-women. We sometimes get in over our heads. But, it turns out, God loves to help us in those times. If we start thinking we are super-hostesses deluxe, we will no doubt fall flat. It's good to be humble, and it's good to keep going even when we don't think we can. We are not to grow weary of showing hospitality, and we are not to grumble about having people over. So that means we have to pace ourselves. If you are tempted to grow weary, take a short break. Ask God to recharge your batteries.

Which leads me to another point.

Get away together occasionally, as you are able. Not because you deserve it, but rather because we all need times of refreshment. Ask God to provide the means for you to have some time away, even if it is just one evening a week for a date. But don't set yourself up for temptation by having high expectations for an amazing getaway. That is a sure way to be disappointed. When we get out of town for a few days, I find that I can't wait to get back and roll up my sleeves.

My husband works fifty or sixty hours a week, and he is always home for dinner. Well, almost always. We have had crunch times where we just hunker down and push through. But those times have been the exception and not the rule. Don't resent your husband's schedule. Remember you are his helper, not his adversary. Be on his team. Help him get help if he needs it. Pray for that assistant. But stick with him and get the schedule under control. Man was not made for the schedule but the schedule for man. Don't forget that.

Finally, don't complain. Be thankful. Overflow in gratitude. That's lots prettier and more effective.

chapter 11

EXPECTATIONS FOR THE

MINISTER'S WIFE

In most congregations, it is common for the minister's wife to be looked up to as a helper, counselor, friend, and guide. This is not because she is herself extraordinarily gifted, but simply because the congregation looks up to the pastor, and so they also want to look up to his wife. This is spiritually healthy, and it gives the minister's wife the right kind of pressure to be learning good things so she can pass them on. In other words, you must be prepared and available for whatever unexpected things come up.

Now, this can be disconcerting. You don't want people expecting more of you than is humanly possible. At the same time, you should realize that it is just the way it goes. It comes with the territory. Women are going to want to look up to you; they are going to expect you to rise to the occasion, whatever that might be. So you may as well brace yourself and get geared up for this because it is inevitable.

I have no idea how many times someone has asked me for advice or help, and I have sent up a silent SOS to God. "Lord, I have no idea where to go with this one. Please help!" He has always answered my prayer. Sometimes the answer is, "Let me talk with Doug and I'll call you back." Other times the Lord may give me a good answer on the spot, so good in fact, that I know it is from Him and obviously not from me.

Here's an example of what I mean by rising to the occasion. Once a family in our congregation had one of their children in the ER, and Doug was out of town. So I went. I am not normally the one to do this, but I loved this family, and I was eager to get there just to be with them. I had no "ministry plan" in mind when I arrived. But when I walked into the room where the family was waiting, one of them said something like, "Thank the Lord. You've come." I quickly realized that, ready or not, they were looking to me expectantly. So I sent up my quick SOS and stepped forward expecting God to do something. I spoke to them, and I prayed with them, and God comforted their hearts. I had no profound words. It was nothing very impressive. But for me it was an example of God's kindness to me. I was comforted by His comfort which He extended both *to me* and *through me*. This was a powerful reminder to me that God will do His work best through me when I am wholly dependent on Him.

So the minister's wife needs to be prepared and available to do things that she may not feel or be very good at or very comfortable doing. This may include welcoming newcomers when you are shy, offering counsel when you feel stupid, visiting the sick when you don't know what to say, showing hospitality far beyond your means, comforting the bereaved when you feel at a loss, or teaching the women in your congregation when you feel like you are the one who needs to be taught.

When I was first engaged to my husband, I remember this hitting me hard. It went something like this: "Oh dear. I am marrying a man who is going to be doing big things. The woman who marries this man is going to be called on to do big things, things which are far bigger than I am. How will I do this? I am just a squirt of a little Christian, not a big impressive one. Ahh. That's the whole point! God will make up all the difference. I am going to have to trust Him. And if He is the One who is leading me to marry this man, then He will equip me to do all those things that terrify me."

This is still true. After all, I'm writing a book for ministers' wives, and I really have no business doing so. But surprisingly, God will use it in spite of me because He is faithful. This is really what living the Christian life means. It's not limited to the experience of ministers' wives, but I believe we have a unique calling that brings many opportunities for us to trust God to do in and through us more than is humanly possible.

But let's go back to the beginning. The congregation wants a minister that they can be proud of. They certainly don't want to be ashamed of the minister. And the same is true of his wife and family. They don't want to point to the wife and the kids as though to say, "Not sure what went wrong here." This does not mean that the minister's family puts on a show. But they should have the mentality that they are to exemplify what the minister is teaching. They are his qualification. They are the example on the chalk-board (whether they like it or not) for the congregation to see. And this does not mean they are pointing to themselves. It simply means that they should not be surprised when other people are doing the pointing. This is where the whole idea of "living in the fish bowl" must come from. We might as well accept this: we need to live in a way that pleases God. Our congregations are going to be watching, and that's okay.

At the same time, I must confess that I have seldom felt like I was living in a fish bowl. Maybe it's because we have always had a remarkably kind congregation. They are considerate and loving toward us and not intrusive or demanding. We love the good people who worship with us every week, and our home has never been Grand Central Station.

Every good wife is a crown to her husband, and the minister's crown is highly visible from the pulpit. Like it or not, this is the way it is. By accepting this fact, I am not suggesting that we ministers' wives think more highly of ourselves than we ought. Far from it. We simply need to be aware that we have a highly visible position in our church, so we ought to make the most of it rather than pretend it is otherwise.

We are not to strive to be the kind of minister's wife that we think our congregation will like. Rather, we should strive to be the kind of minister's wife that the minister will like. And, thankfully, if we strive for the latter, the former will (hopefully!) happen of its own accord. That doesn't mean the minister's wife will be the most popular woman in the church (as though we even think in such silly categories). But it means that if we are working hard to be a good wife to our husband, then the congregation will be blessed as a result, which will result in the minister's wife being well-loved and well-liked. We women often want to strive to be liked first. But the "being liked" part is a consequence of sticking to our first duties first, and not the other way around.

One more thing. The minister's wife should want to be a good "advertisement" for her husband. The way a wife looks speaks volumes about the man she is married to. So be a good advertisement. Dress in a manner that he is pleased with. Don't be frumpy and don't be frivolous. Strive for the happy medium. (Well, maybe a tad above medium!) I have had the experience over the years of meeting wives of ministers who bear the sad tell-tale signs of neglect. They look unloved and it shows. This is a sign of the minister's failure to lead and love his wife, and so I do not "blame" the wife. It is the husband's responsibility to bestow loveliness on his wife. Meanwhile, it is the duty of the minister's wife to be a responsive and loving recipient of her husband's love, and as a result, to be the kind of woman the congregation can appreciate and look up to.

chapter 12

SUNDAY

MORNING

For nine years while our kids were growing up, my husband left the house on Sunday mornings very early to drive thirty miles and preach for another congregation before returning to our service. During those first couple years, I was not so very fond of Sunday. It was a tough day for me. But I was grateful he got out the door in the morning without having to discipline kids or change diapers. I was grateful he could stay focused on his duties. I would fix him breakfast and send him out the door.

Sunday meant getting my house ready to be a drop-off nursery. We were meeting in a body and paint shop (honest!) with no suitable room on site for the little ones. So I got things put away and set up, and then the moms took turns each week supervising the nursery. I got the three kids dressed, fed, and loaded into the car, and then off we went to church. Sometimes (I can't remember why) I had to find a ride, so I especially disliked calling around asking friends if they could give the four of us a ride to church.

During this era, a friend of mine casually commented to me that she looked forward to Sunday all week long. It was her favorite day. I was completely startled. I probably turned red. I realized with a shock that here I was, the pastor's wife, and I did not share her attitude about Sunday.

This was a pretty big turning point for me. I repented of the self-pity party that I had been throwing myself on Sunday mornings, and I began to ask God to adjust my attitude and to help me think about Sunday the way I knew I should. After that Sundays started to become something more than just a weekly hurdle to get over. I still had the business of getting the kids to church by myself, but I began to see the significance of what I was doing and how important it was. That was the beginning of the overhaul God would do on my view of His day.

chapter 13

PREPARING FOR THE

LORD'S DAY

The weekly high point for all the saints is the Lord's Day, but this is particularly the case in a minister's home. This is what he has been gearing up for all week, and it is the culmination of much preparation, prayer, and anticipation. For wives, we might compare it to a week of preparation for a feast: first we plan the menu, then we gather the ingredients; next we cook the food, and finally we serve it up to the crowd. This is exhilarating, but also exhausting, work. And it is good work.

A pastor has many commitments and interruptions to fill his week: counseling appointments, studying, thinking (if he has time), reading, assembling his thoughts into a sermon, meetings, emails and phone calls. I hope you see how crucial it is that in the midst of all these demanding duties that someone is praying for him, encouraging him, and helping him to reach the finish line (Sunday morning) in good shape to preach a sermon. Of course, that someone is you, the pastor's wife. By this I do not mean that a woman is responsible in any ultimate way for her husband's spiritual well-being. But on the other hand, she has much power in her hand to bring him good (Proverbs 31:12), and she ought to be dishing out the good stuff all week long with a sharp eye out for Sunday.

The minister's wife has a unique duty and opportunity to minister to the saints by means of ministering to her husband. As she thinks about and prepares for him, she is equipping him to discharge his duties to the congregation. This means all the basic things I've already mentioned like keeping him clothed and fed. But it also means keeping a lookout for when he seems over-tired, under-encouraged, or just simply spent. She has a good vantage point on these things and should use all her powers to keep his batteries charged. This is the minister's wife's most important duty in her service to God. A pastor who is ministered to at home will be enabled to minister to his congregation. But a pastor who is neglected or forgotten in his own home will be ill equipped to help anyone.

Sometimes the minister's wife has so many of her own distractions and duties that her husband can be (not intentionally) overlooked. After all, he is an adult and can pour his own cheerios in the bowl, unlike all the short people in the household. And a wife may be so exhausted with her own labors in the home that she is in poor shape to minister to her husband. This requires wisdom. She may need to make some changes so that she can still focus on the man she was designed to help and who needs her desperately. A man may be able to handle a certain amount of neglect, but after a while he will cave in some area or other. By all means, if you are an overworked mother who doesn't have time to minister to your husband, get housecleaning, babysitting, homeschooling, or cooking help (or all of the above). Talk with your husband about how to lighten your load so you can lighten his.

This neglect can also surface if you are too busy with teaching Sunday school, organizing the nursery, or being involved in some other church-related ministry like hospitality. Be careful you don't neglect your first calling by taking on secondary responsibilities, even if they are worthy duties in themselves. Someone has said, "The need is not the call" and this is very true. Don't overload yourself with extra duties that will make you ineffective in your home. Remember that "pastor's wife" is not a church office. You are not the church secretary or the church hostess, even if some in the church think you are. You are a wife. This is a full-time job, no matter what the world says or thinks. And if we want to really get good at this before we die, then we are going to have to devote some real thought, energy, and practice into it.

As the week rolls around to its close, it is prime time to pay attention to the minister. Have you been helping him through the week? Have you been giving to him sexually? There is still time. Have you been attentive to his other needs? Are there areas where he needs your help but you have failed to notice? We need to pay attention to these things. And we must bathe the upcoming Lord's Day in prayer. Saturday is a good time to be praying for Sunday morning. It is also a good time to get hit with temptation, so be wary. An obviously good strategy of the devil's is to get the pastor out of fellowship with his wife on Saturday so he is not in good shape on Sunday. We must be alert to these things and not forget we have an enemy.

The wife can do some very mundane, practical things on Saturday to prepare for the Lord's Day. She can have her husband's clothes in order so that there is no scramble for socks or an ironed shirt. She can know what she is going to prepare him for breakfast. And speaking of breakfast, she should give her husband some fuel on the Lord's Day because he is going to be expending a lot of energy in the pulpit. Sabbath breakfast can be part of your weekly celebration. Maybe it's the only morning you do a full-tilt breakfast of eggs and bacon or pancakes. If so, this will take some preparation Saturday night if you are going to pull it off Sunday a.m. Get in the habit. Make it a regular ritual.

If your home includes children, whether big or little, few or many, Sunday morning can be hectic. Keeping the children busy and cheerful is another way a wife can help her husband as he prepares himself for his duties. The children need to be prepared for the Lord's Day as well. They must be taught that what their father does on Sunday is very important. They should not take his calling lightly, but see that it is an enormous privilege and blessing to have a minister for a father. Of course this is impossible if Sunday morning is a hassle. The children should love to see the Lord's Day arrive, and their mother should do all she can to make it a wonderful morning of getting ready.

For example, each child can have special duties and privileges on this day. It doesn't have to be anything elaborate.

For example one family I know serves what they call "Sabbath milk" on Sunday morning, which is whole milk. The rest of the week they drink 2%. This same family celebrates in the afternoon with ice cream sundaes, and the children get to put all different kinds of toppings on their ice cream. This makes their Lord's Day celebration a joy, and they treasure these simple Sunday traditions. It doesn't have to be complicated.

We wives can do more than we realize to make Sunday morning a smooth, sweet time for our husbands. We want to send him off to church in a hassle-free manner, not harried out the door in the wake of grumbling or fussing. As we pray for our husbands and for the upcoming Sunday, part of our prayers should be devoted to this idea of sending him out filled and fattened, not strained and starved.

Each home is unique just as each pastor is unique. The family culture that will grow up around the Lord's Day and how it is celebrated will vary from home to home. Some pastors want to have guests over after church for a big meal. Some want to relax and put their feet up for the afternoon and take a nap without having extra people in their home. A wise wife will adapt her style to his needs and know what will be the greatest help to him. If there is an evening service where the minister is preaching a second sermon, he may need some rest in between. This is not forsaking his duties, but rather preparing for them. If the afternoon is filled with people, people, people, he may be too burned out to preach with effectiveness. On the other hand, he may be the kind of man who is rejuvenated with lots of people around. Though many of the saints do and should practice hospitality on the Lord's Day, the minister's home may be in need of rest on some Sundays and open for company on others. The important thing is to be flexible and open to the possibilities; we should not feel guilty if we are resting on the Lord's Day.

Finally, the Lord's Day should end just as it began: with sweetness and rest. Our husbands need to know that they are a blessing to us. Comforting words and gracious speech are required all the time, but what better way to begin the new week than with gratitude and kindness? Our husbands need to hear that we are grateful for their ministry to us, to our children, and to the saints. The day should be surrounded with a hedge of thanksgiving that we wives are careful to express. We should honor them for their faithful labor and hard work always, but even more so on the Lord's Day.

Okay, so now I have thoroughly convicted myself! I am so glad I reminded myself of all these things. It isn't too late. Sunday is coming and I have another week to have a shot at it. God is so gracious to give us so many chances to make it up. Each week we confess our sins and shortcomings, and He gives us a whole, fresh week to try it again. So pour it on and bless your husband. Don't give it up after one good week and don't give up after a failed attempt. Determine to make it a pattern in that gets richer and deeper week after week.

chapter 14

BEARING BURDENS OR

HEAVY LIFTING

Let's look at a few more of the duties that come with being a minister's wife. Of course it all depends on your gifts and opportunities and just exactly what your husband wants you to do. But it's important to remember first principles: you cannot export what you don't have at home. If your own home is a wreck, you cannot go out and teach the young women how to keep their homes. If your children are undisciplined, you cannot be a source of wisdom on childrearing. But if you have your priorities straight, if your own house is in order, if your marriage is healthy and your spiritual life is growing, then you do have something to export and you ought to be sharing it. The standard is not perfection; if that were the case, then no one would be fit to minister to anyone else. So we don't need to wait around until we are in perfect order since that will never happen. But neither do we want to be helping tend other people's gardens when our own is needy.

Having said that, I really believe there are unique obligations and responsibilities that come with being a minister's wife. A minister's wife needs to be able to bear some heavy burdens. At any given time, your husband may be involved in a number of difficult situations, most of which you cannot talk about with anyone else. Sometimes they happen all at once, and they may come at any time day or night. He may be resolving marriage or family conflicts, visiting sick folks at the hospital, standing at death beds, comforting the bereaved, visiting someone in jail, or helping people make very difficult decisions. If the minister's wife is going to help bear the burdens that her husband carries, she is going to have to learn how to process these things.

You can bear burdens in an unhelpful way when you become worrisome, when you are constantly asking your husband about someone, when you are lying awake at night fretting over someone else's problems. Bearing burdens does not mean worrying over them. It means praying, helping, and trusting them to God. Remember it is their marriage, not yours, that is having problems. Keep your perspective. Bearing burdens with your husband means that you can keep a confidence. It means you are a sounding board for your husband when and if he needs one. It means you are open to help out any way you can. Sometimes it is a bigger help to stay out of the way. Other times your husband may want you to come with him to the hospital or to counsel someone. But you can write a note, send a message, make a meal, or find other ways to support the people who are needy in your congregation. These are ways you are helping him be a good minister.

A minister's calling is not like a nine-to-five job; it is his life. I find it is best not to keep track of his hours, but I know that my husband has seldom put in a forty-hour work week. It is far beyond that. He has a couple of early morning meetings a week; he has a couple of monthly evening meetings; and then there are the emergencies that come up without notice. He works in the church office Monday through Friday, and he takes Saturday off. Sunday he fills the pulpit. He officiates at weddings and conducts funerals. This is the minister's calling.

I believe a minister's wife can get derailed if she reacts wrongly to her husband's schedule. Remember that his life is your life; his calling is your calling. You are to identify with him in all that he is doing. You are both in the ministry together. He may be the one up front, but you are the one supporting him and encouraging him and sticking with him.

Sometimes a wife can become detached rather than involved in what her husband is doing. This may seem like self-defense. She thinks that if she never really expects him to be around, she won't be disappointed if he isn't. So she gives him over to the church and abandons him there. But that's not what he needs. Another unhelpful response to a husband's busy schedule is to become bitter at the people who need his help, to keep tabs on his hours, and to feel resentful that he doesn't spend more time at home. This is far from helpful too. And some wives may feel they are being spiritual when they are pushing their husbands out the door to "go minister." He may need to be home.

Being a minister's wife is a sweet calling. You have a close view of God's providence in the lives of many people, a closer view than most Christian women get. Sometimes it is a bittersweet calling that requires bearing the heavy burdens of those in your congregation. As I write this, my husband is at the hospital, helping a young couple bear the heavy burden of a newborn child who will soon die. A minister's wife participates in these things, bearing her husband up in prayer as he bears others up.

So a minister's wife needs to know how to minister alongside her husband as a fellow soldier of Jesus Christ. That does not necessarily mean that she will always be on the front lines; sometimes she is working behind the scenes, supplying her husband with fresh resources, whether by praying for him or by preparing a meal or getting his suit cleaned. She is his co-worker and co-laborer. She works alongside him, doing whatever she can as she sees need.

We should count ourselves blessed to be married to men who preach the Word faithfully with boldness and authority, who sacrifice for their congregations, giving us a good (and close-up) example to follow. It is an honor, a privilege, and a high calling to be a minister's wife. It requires faith and courage and self-denial. It means freely lending your husband to others so that he might minister to them, even if he is late for dinner.

chapter 15

CHEERLEADING OR KEEPING OUR

PERSPECTIVE

My husband has been in the pulpit nearly every Lord's Day for thirty-five years. It's hard to imagine a life where I am not in the front row listening to him preach every Sunday. Of course I've heard many other ministers over the years, and we have visited many other churches, but usually (not always) when we are visiting, my husband is in the pulpit. All this is to say, he has probably preached around 1,750 sermons, if I had been keeping count.

Given that he does this every week, it is possible to forget the strategic importance of my husband's work. The food just appears on the table, week after week. We get up and go to church and come home again. If we are not careful, we wives can reduce our view of the ministry to a job with a paycheck. We can gradually become blasé about what it is our husbands are actually doing. After all, he does this same thing every Sunday, fifty weeks out of the year, and he's been doing it for decades. The *routine* of weekly meetings and sermon prep and Sunday mornings can distract us away from remembering the momentousness of our husbands' calling. We can get more concerned about what's in the oven for dinner than whether he is prepared to preach the Word. We can begin to see it as mostly trying to keep everyone in the congregation happy by inviting the right people to dinner, visiting with the right people after the service, making sure the minister has his tie on straight, and making sure the minister and his family are presentable and appropriately attired. This reduces the ministry into a dreary humdrum of people-pleasing.

If God's worship is central to our lives, and we know it is, then we wives had better stay alert to our husband's part in it. Preaching has momentous consequences each week, for good or ill. It is not trivial, but vital. It is not insignificant, but crucial. It is a heavy burden for our husbands to bear, and yet God gives strength. When our husbands step into the pulpit each week, we should expect great things to happen in our own hearts and lives as well as in those in the assembled congregation. This is something we absolutely must not ever forget or take for granted.

Like Martha, we can become distracted. Someone forgot to clean the ladies' bathroom! Someone didn't announce the ladies' prayer meeting! Someone didn't vote to give the pastor a raise! Someone is wearing something way too zingy to church! You get the idea.

If we understand the burdens our husbands carry as they faithfully preach the Word, we will pray for them. We won't take it lightly or get distracted. We'll set our minds on things above. We'll pray for these men and ask God to help us as we help them. God has designed us and called us to do this. These faithful men need faithful helpers. Far from being blasé about what our husbands do, we can be enthusiastic and eager to see what God will do again this week. God has kindly given us a new day, a new week, to try again, to refocus and reboot. Let's do better next time!

chapter 16

COUNSELING IN THE

CHURCH

One thing that seems to come with the territory for the pastor's wife is counseling women in the congregation. I have never hung out a shingle, but I have always tried to make myself available to help if I can. Of course I've learned many things along the way. Here are a few principles I suggest you use in counseling.

1. The first important point to remember is this: you are not the pastor. In fact, you are not even an elder. Many women need the kind of help that you can offer, but some will have more involved troubles that require pastoral oversight. You should be careful to know the difference and feel free to hand things off to the pastoral staff at your church. (For some of you, that may mean handing it off to your husband. I know! I did that for years.)

2. Don't be tempted to think that you can or should solve all the women's problems in the church (or any of them, for

that matter). Neither should you feel guilty that you cannot. God has not equipped you for such things. This work belongs to the pastor and elders. This is not to underrate the work you can do in teaching, exhorting, and helping women. But it is important to know that the responsibility of shepherding the flock lies not with you, but with the elders. All the tough problems should be handed off to them.

Of course some of you may be trained in biblical counseling, and if so, then that is a wonderful blessing. I am not saying here that women cannot counsel. I am simply encouraging you to avail yourself of help if you need it. Don't feel that you must give counsel if you don't feel equipped or prepared to do so. If you are reluctant, maybe you just need a nudge. Many problems can be solved by teaching basic Christian principles, so I urge you to give it a try!

Sometimes women prefer to speak to another woman rather than with the pastor or one of the elders, and there could be several legitimate reasons. First, she may be too intimidated by the thought of meeting with them. Or perhaps she simply feels more comfortable speaking with you. As long as she understands that you will be passing the information on to your husband, this is fine.

On the other hand, sometimes a woman does not want the kind of accountability for her words and actions that the elders can provide, so she may say she would rather meet with you. The main thing here is to exercise wisdom. Do not allow yourself to be manipulated. A woman may feel free to "let it all hang out" with you, but would exercise far more wisdom and caution in speaking with the elders. Be cautious yourself in such circumstances. Your husband should be able to direct you through this kind of situation, as in all the others.

3. The next important principle is never to speak for the elders. If a woman asks you what the elders would do in a certain situation, be very careful in your reply. Be deferential toward them and assure her that they will seek to act wisely and prudently. But do not commit them to any particular course of action. It is always better to say, "I do not know and cannot speak for them."

4. This next one may sound weird, but hear me out. Always give counsel on your terms, not on the terms of the woman in distress. Of course your terms should have a biblical frame of reference, but you must never allow yourself to become dominated by other people's troubles. For example, you must never promise to keep anything from your husband. If a woman asks you to promise you will not tell anyone what she is about to disclose, do not agree to such a promise. Tell her you will exercise a responsible confidentiality, but let her know that you never keep anything from your husband. Furthermore, he may (or may not) feel it is necessary to inform the elders. You never know what sort of thing she is going to tell you, and you do not want to be put in a situation where you will have to break your word.

5. Do not let women in need of counsel run your schedule. Of course there are always emergencies. I'm not speaking of that right now. But if a woman is *always* having an emergency, you must learn to say no. You have duties and responsibilities, and you must be a good steward of your

time. Schedule your appointments and phone calls. Let her know if this is not a good time. If she is upset, it may give her time to cool off. If she is in great need, and it's a bad time for you, tell her exactly how much time you have to talk. If she knows you only have ten minutes, she will summarize her difficulty. If you always give way and allow for interruptions all day long, that is exactly what you will continue to have. It is usually easy to tell what kind of woman you are dealing with. Some are very reluctant to intrude into your day and are very gracious. Others begin talking before finding out if you are busy. But if you are disciplined and orderly in your counseling, you will be able to manage it along with everything else. Some women may become too dependent on you if you are not careful. Be wise in knowing how often to meet and how long each meeting should be (I recommend one hour max). Make sure they understand that "you" are not the answer. Agree to meet a couple of times and see how it's going before you sign up for more.

6. Next, when a woman comes for help, give her something concrete to do. Perhaps she needs to apologize to her husband or children for something. You may suggest that she do something to show respect to her husband. Perhaps she needs to confess some things to God or make restitution of some kind. Give her an assignment, and then next time you talk with her, ask her if she did it. This will tell you whether she is really seeking counsel or if she just wants to talk. If she refuses to do what you ask, then you should refuse to see her again until she does. This keeps the relationship on the right track so that you do not become a dumping ground for her problems. We always want to offer

sound, godly, biblical counsel to women rather than mere "counseling" that can easily drift into an unprofitable habit, or become an opportunity to "vent" rather than a means of bringing about real change and growth.

7. Find out if this woman has already gone for counsel elsewhere. Maybe she has already asked her husband's advice but she doesn't want to follow it. This is important to know before you dive in. Sometimes women will go from one person to the other seeking sympathy, but as soon as the counsel begins to require something of them, they look elsewhere. You may be the latest in a long chain of "counselors." The goal is to bring about real solid help. It is not to spend hours and hours talking with no real result. Some women really do enjoy hearing themselves vent, and the more they tell the story over and over, the worse it really does get. There is a weird sort of pleasure in this kind of self-pity. Do not be a party to such things.

8. Keep in mind that there are always two sides to every story. When you speak to a woman, keep the conversation centered on *her* problems, not her husband's. You and she cannot fix his problems. Keep bringing the subject back to her behavior, her demeanor, her sin, and her responsibility in the situation. Tell her that whoever speaks to her husband can speak to him about his problems. Your duty is to speak to her about hers.

9. Don't allow your counseling load to overtake you or keep you from your domestic duties. If it becomes overwhelming, you may need to be handing far more of it off

to other women or to the elders. Perhaps you have let some women intrude into your life more than they should have. Take responsibility for this. Are you really giving good counsel, or are you allowing yourself to be used unprofitably?

10. Sometimes I have "lost" a woman because she has not liked what I have told her. She doesn't want to come back because I was too hard on her. Of course, if you think you have given ungodly counsel or given it in an ungodly manner, go back and seek forgiveness. But you should not determine whether or not your counsel was good counsel based on the reaction. Some women react positively and obediently to God's Word; others reject it and turn away. The response is not your problem.

11. One word about email counseling. I have done a little bit of this, and it is very difficult. Beware getting sucked into difficult cases with people you do not know and cannot meet. People will often write in an email things they would never dare to speak out loud. Offer what you can and then suggest pastoral help if possible. If there is not a good church in their area, perhaps you can suggest an elder in your church that is willing to help. Our church has one elder who does this kind of counseling.

12. Always tell the truth. Be kind and compassionate, but be willing to address sin and disobedience openly. Do not think you must qualify everything or apologize for telling the truth. Some women ask me if I have ever had the same problem. I tell them as gently as I can that my experience is not the issue. We are trying to get to the more important issue, which is what God's Word says about her

situation. It is not whether my husband or I have sinned in the same way. I believe this is just a way of seeking reassurance. Try to offer hope and comfort without going into your own history. That is not the point of counseling. On the other hand, if part of your story will be of great use, go ahead and tell it. But don't seek to be "transparent" so that women can relate to you. We don't have to be experienced in every kind of sin to offer help.

13. Make sure you and your husband discuss these things and establish terms and times for your counseling. Your husband is the pastor and is ultimately responsible for all these situations. Don't allow yourself to be kept up late at night worrying over other people's troubles. This has two problems: the first one is that you are not trusting God, and the second one is that worrying assumes that you are the one to fix their troubles. And remember their troubles are not your troubles. Though we should be compassionate and prayerful, we must not become worn down and agitated over other people's troubles. Give them to God. And then trust Him to use you to help those women who come to you.

chapter 17

WOMEN'S MINISTRY IN

THE CHURCH

Before I was married, I was working with a Christian student organization as well as working in a Christian evangelism ministry, so I felt like I was giving myself to "Christian work," and I was. After I was married and settled down to have children, I sometimes wondered what had happened to my "ministry" and when would I get to "minister" again. God kindly dealt with my discontent over this by showing me that I had a very important ministry at home. As my mother-in-law said to me once, "You have three in your congregation." I was involved in full-time Christian work. In fact, more full-time than ever!

Once our children were a bit older, I was able to lead women's Bible studies or help organize some of the ladies' fellowship events. But this was not out of a sense of obligation as the minister's wife. Years later when Bible studies came about, it was a joy to teach them. But I'm very grateful for those years of waiting when I was focused on more important things like ironing and canning and making bread. That was my training ground. Only then did I have something to say! When we rush ahead of God and assume duties He has not given us, we will not find His blessing on our labors. I had important work to do helping my husband, and he needed me to be doing it and not something else.

Over the years I have occasionally asked my husband if he wanted me to lead a women's study, and he would reply, "Do you want to?" In other words, he always wanted me to do this because I wanted to, not out of any sense of guilt. It was a "get to" not a "have to." This has helped me immensely. If I would like to lead a study, I do. If I feel that I'm too busy at the moment, I don't. At the same time, as an older Christian woman, I do have a duty (not as a pastor's wife, but as an older woman) to reach out to the younger women. And it so happens that I love doing so.

Most congregations have some kind of organized ladies' fellowship, but just whose responsibility is it to oversee and organize it? The answer may seem obvious, but just like all the other ministries in the church, it is the elders' responsibility to oversee it. They are accountable to God for the life and health of the church and all its members, including the women. So they may delegate it to responsible women in the church, and this may or may not include the pastor's wife. Remember, the women are not her congregation, and she is not their pastor. At the same time, it may be a great help if she can minister to the women. But there are many other things to consider. For example, what are the ages of her children? Does she have time for this, given her commitments at home? Will it put too much pressure on her?

Not all pastors' wives are gifted teachers or organizers, nor want to be. She should not feel inferior or guilty if she is not leading the women. It may be that this is just not the time.

Whatever her ministry to the women looks like, the pastor's wife should be modeling to the women in her church what a joyful wife looks like and how a home can be a blessed place for a husband to come home to. This is her first and her most important calling. All other ministry flows from this.

chapter 18

THE BENEFITS

We all agree there are many challenges that face the wife of a minister. It's easy to concentrate on the hard things because those are the things that stretch and challenge us. Sometimes we need a boost up, and it's always nice to know we aren't alone, that other minister's wives are going through the same kinds of difficulties with us. Since I addressed some of the heavy lifting the minster's wife does, I thought it might be good to consider the benefits of being married to a minister. *Are there any benefits?* Yes, of course there are many benefits, blessings, and privileges that come with being married to a faithful, godly minister. So I've devoted this section to the benefits that may have slipped our minds while we were busy being hunkered down, riding out the rough spots.

First of all, a woman who marries a minister shares in his calling. If he is called to be a minister, then she is called to be his helper in this ministry, and that is indeed a remarkable privilege in itself. Though all lawful vocations are a means of glorifying God, the minister has a unique position, and his wife is called to walk with him in this.

The minister's wife is a suitable helper, a true companion for her husband, whether she really feels qualified or not. God must have thought so or He would not have sent her to help a minister. And, as his helper, she has many opportunities that the other wives in the congregation do not share. She should not shrink back from these, but embrace the opportunities she has to be a fellow laborer, co-worker, and co-soldier with her husband. As his helper, her duties may take her into many situations where she can see first-hand God's grace exhibited through her husband. She has a bird's-eye view.

The minister's wife stands at the graveside while her husband ministers the Word to the grieving; she sits at weddings as he pronounces over the joy of the couple. Often she is there with him at bedsides, in hospitals, funeral homes, or visiting grieving families. A minister's wife is in many ways an apprentice, learning to extend comfort, help, and solace in ways she never anticipated. She learns the Scriptures from her husband as he teaches from the Word, applying it to those in need, in all kinds of situations.

A minister's wife has an unusual vantage point, participating as she does in her husband's ministry to the saints. Though many in the congregation may share in these things, few have as many opportunities as the minister and his wife. This is her discipleship. Seeing God working in the lives of the congregation is a huge blessing and benefit for her own spiritual life and growth. God's Word is not just theoretical, but immensely practical.

The minister's wife also has the privilege of sitting under her husband's preaching in season and out, week after week, in all kinds of situations. One of my favorite quotes comes from George Whitefield: "I love those who thunder out the Word. The Christian world is in a deep sleep! Nothing but a loud voice can awaken them out of it." Though it is a blessing to be married to a minister, it is a far greater blessing to be married to a minister who thunders out the Word courageously and without fear. We should remind our husbands every week to "thunder away!"

Not everyone is married to their pastor. Funny when you think about it! I know my husband values my input and feedback, but I am in no position to offer criticism because I am too busy being fed! Still, I do ask questions, take notes, and thank him for the good sermon. And I do on occasion offer a suggestion. But his preaching is food for my soul, not food for criticism.

Not only does the minister's wife get to sit under her husband's teaching, she also has the uncommon privilege of helping prepare him to stand in the pulpit week after week. It takes more than just the sermon prep. We wives are more necessary than we know. They couldn't do it without us. Now that is a big blessing: to be needed by a man of God!

If I am helping my husband, then I am participating in his ministry. And that is good. I don't want to be an elder or a pastor. I don't want to stand in the pulpit and preach. That is not my calling. (And I say, hallelujah and amen!) But what a privilege it is to do my part to make it easy for him to fulfill his obligations. We really must not underestimate the great work our husbands do in preaching the Word. If we have the eye of faith, we will see that God is doing wonderful things by means of His ministers. And what a joy it is to participate from the sidelines, cheering our husbands on as they preach the Word with boldness and faith.

Another great advantage of being married to a minister is the life of faith you share together. Ministering together requires consistent application of faith and cannot be done without prayer and time in the Word. Coasting does not work for the minister or his wife. She can't afford to be a slacker. And what a great impetus: to be a good helper for a minister means growing in grace, growing in the Word, and growing in faithfulness and good works.

PART 4

Challenges & Trials

chapter 19

WHEN THE MINISTER

NEEDS HELP

One of the obvious duties of the minister is to counsel and encourage his congregation when they are in the midst of hard times. Even the families who may not know the pastor very well should feel free to call on him when they have a trouble. The minister is available to help when someone is ill, when there's a death, when there is bad news, when there are marriage troubles or family troubles, or any other kind of sticky situation. And the minister's wife may be involved in some of these things. She should make herself available, depending on her own situation and family responsibilities, to help the women in her congregation who need her input, advice, comfort, or counsel.

But who will minister to the pastor and his wife when they are the ones having difficulties? Now I'm not talking here about when the pastor loses a loved one. I believe most congregations are in the best position to help and comfort his family at such a time. But what about if the problem is related to his family? Maybe one of his kids is struggling. Whom can they call for help? This is a dilemma that happens far more often than we realize. If a pastor's family is having a hard time, they may feel like they have to go it alone. What else can they do? In many cases, the trouble may have to do with the church itself, and it would be unwise for the pastor to call on someone in the congregation, because that would put the church member in a difficult position. Perhaps the minister feels like he is not allowed to have troubles (not part of the job description). He may feel a pressure to be trouble-free in the eyes of the congregation. After all, he is teaching them how to live, so he had better be an example of all that he is teaching.

Even so, ministers often do need help, and having a committee in the church designated as a support team may not actually provide the kind of support he really needs. And it's not anyone's fault. The minister may need a sounding-board, he may need advice and prayer, or he may need counsel. But how can he involve someone in his congregation without making that person a "player"? Or, if he has one elder with whom he can confide, how can he keep it from looking like an exclusive club? Sometimes the best place to get help and support is from a fellow minister from another congregation in another county rather than from a friend in the congregation, no matter how dear he may be.

Cultivating friendships with other ministers, even if they are in other states, is healthy and wise. This can provide for helpful counsel and input, can take some of the pressure off, and will keep the pastor from being a burden to his own people. This is one of the reasons why I appreciate ministers' conferences: the ministers get time to be together, to talk shop, and to enjoy the fellowship of their peers.

Wives, as much as is possible, should do the same, and cultivate friendships with other minister's wives, even if they are in different denominations. This does not mean that I think a minister's wife should not have dear friends in her own church. Of course she should. But there is something very comforting about being able to enjoy the fellowship of another pastor's wife who knows something of life in the ministry. The reality is that sometimes no one really wants to be too close of friends with the minister or his wife. I have heard it commonly shared among ministers' wives that they are seldom invited into the homes of their congregation. This just comes with the territory and should not be viewed necessarily as a failure on the part of the pastor. There is just something intimidating about having the pastor over, so don't blame the folks in your congregation if this is the case. And don't blame yourself either.

So cultivate friendships with women who are in different churches, and ministers' wives who serve in different congregations. It may be refreshing to have friends who are not looking to you with any kind of expectation. There may come a time when you and your husband need someone to give you a fresh perspective on some tangle, and it will be helpful to get an outside viewpoint. My husband and I have the great privilege of having many friends in the ministry around the country. We know we could call them if we needed help, and they feel the same way about us. This does not in any way undermine the close friendships we have in our congregation. I think it improves them!

chapter 20

WHEN FRIENDS

LEAVE

One of the blessings associated with being a minister's wife is meeting people from many walks of life, and then growing to love all these people. As your husband (and you) minister to them, many of these folks will become very dear to you, and this is a very great blessing. But when some of these same people leave your church to attend another one, it can be painful or confusing. As with most everything in the world, we can either respond wisely or foolishly, and since this is not something that happens rarely, we should have a biblical perspective of church membership so we can respond in a God-honoring way.

First, let me say that over the years I have probably experienced the gamut of emotions over this one. As a young minister's wife, I was not at all prepared for this to happen. In fact, I don't believe that it had ever occurred to me that good friends would up and go. So it came as a surprise (shock) the first time it happened, and I took it very personally, getting my feelings hurt in the process. And that really just muddies the water and doesn't help at all, so I don't recommend it.

People change. They may have loved your church and even helped get it started back in the day. But loyalties shift and people go through hard times. Sometimes they think changing churches will help them get a fresh start; sometimes they think the church is the cause of their problems; sometimes it's just that a new preacher has come to town and he is the happening thing. Did any of your current members come to your church from another one across town? How did you take it back then? Were you concerned with how they left their old church and their former pastor? Or did you assume they were wise in leaving their church to come to yours? You might want to think about this and the Golden Rule.

Sometimes it is a friendly departure with appropriate farewells and blessings exchanged; sometimes it is disruptive and careless; sometimes old friends leave without a word. Each person will have a different story to tell about leaving your church, so don't be surprised by anything.

What helps us keep the right perspective is remembering that the church belongs to Jesus Christ, not to us. Our own individual church is not the only one in the world. Our husbands are not the only men who can teach and preach. It's a big world. My father told me many times as I was growing up that you can please some of the people some of the time, but you cannot ever please all the people all the time. So it is important for us to keep our eye on this important detail:

We serve God and we want to please Him. We can never make everyone happy.

When people come and go, we must realize this is nothing new. I used to joke with a friend of mine whose husband was a minister in a neighboring town that we should get some kind of board with colored pins to keep track of who was at which church. (Our members went back and forth quite a bit back then.) Joking with her about this helped us both keep relaxed about it all. We were not competing for membership. We were not trying to be the most popular church back then, nor are we now. Life is too short to fuss over such things. The thing we are striving for is faithfulness, not numbers. But faithfulness brings growth with it. And growth is sometimes measured differently than we expect. God prunes the tree to cause more fruitfulness. He cuts off dead branches and He grafts others in. When you think about it, the whole thing is a deep mystery.

You may be in one of those difficult situations where people are not just leaving, but they are leaving mad. And they are mad because of something you said or mad at your husband or the session for how they handled some situation or other. I am truly sorry. If you feel betrayed, hurt, or even peeved about it, I have to say that I really do understand that this is not fun.

At the same time, you have to remind yourself that your church belongs to God. It's not even named after you, it is named after Him. He is the Sovereign One and He rules the earth. He overrules evil for good, He works all things for good for His people, and He will never leave you or forsake you. Remind yourself of these precious truths. And then you can thank Him for even this.

Over the years I have seen people leave our church for many different reasons, some good and some poor. But I always appreciate the person who lets us know that he is leaving and why and says goodbye and thanks for everything. It is much easier to see that person leave than the one who was in the church for a decade and then disappeared without a word, or the one who left and opened up a website of accusations against the church on his way out.

Sometimes the person who leaves most carelessly is the one your husband ministered to in extraordinary ways. This is just one more reason to minister to one and all with no strings attached. We do not go the distance for people because we hope they will go the distance for us. No. We minister in Jesus' name, looking to heaven for our reward.

When friends are leaving the church, this is a time for the minister's wife to offer strong support to her husband. Keep him encouraged. If those leaving are making a stink as they go, my counsel to you is to not get embroiled in any controversy. Stay up to speed as your husband keeps you posted, but be content to let the elders deal with it. Keep your emotions in check. *Do not take it personally.* Give these people to God and let them go freely. Don't stir up more trouble by talking about it too much. It is not the end of the world! The work will go on! And sometimes, the work will carry on more effectively without them. As you look back later, you will see how God was bringing good to you and to the church, though you couldn't see it at the time.

All these things season us and bring experience, maturity, and wisdom to our ministry and faith. God uses it all to equip us to be more effective in what He has called us to do. So it makes no sense to become paralyzed by hard feelings or hurt feelings. We must view it in light of God's sovereign purposes and plans that He has for us. We can walk confidently in the good works He has prepared in advance for us.

Church members do not belong to us, and when they leave, sin is not necessarily present, though it could be. Sometimes it is. Sometimes it isn't. But it is foolish to get into a sinful attitude yourself over someone else's perceived or real sin. Focus on the people who are still in the congregation. They still have many needs. Give yourself away to them in Christ's love. Focus on your husband and continue to minister to him. He hasn't changed, and he's not leaving his post.

chapter 21

FRIENDSHIPS

One of the things I hear from time to time is that ministers and their wives can feel lonely. This may seem odd because to others standing by it seems that the minister and his wife know everyone and are overwhelmed with friendships left and right. But that may be an illusion. Reality is that most people want to keep a bit of a distance from the minister, and therefore, also from his wife. So you may have many acquaintances, but few friends.

If you feel that way, then let me encourage you. First of all, let's start with the possibility that you are misinterpreting things. If you're feeling lonely, some of this might be in your own imagination. It may be a hormonal swing that will disappear in a few days. You may have lots of friends, but they've just gotten busy lately. So don't be too hard on everyone and take up the "nobody likes me" tune. This may simply be a temptation to get you down and out. Resist it!

On the other hand, maybe you really are excluded, and you're not making this up. In that case, I suggest that you pray about this first, and then take the initiative. Make a new friend. Have someone over. Reach out. But you may say, "I do that day in and day out!" I didn't say to have a needy person over. Rather, have someone over who isn't "needy." (Although, let's face it, everyone is needy, and the reason we are talking about this is because you are feeling needy at this moment!) Invite someone for coffee or lunch. Get out a little. This may be just what you need to lift your spirits. And often, that's the bottom line: it's our spirits that get a little needy, and we have it in our power to lift them up all by ourselves.

Everyone needs friends, and the minister's wife is no exception. We want our congregations to be communities characterized by sweet fellowship and sacrificial living, and that means that we will be all tangled up in one another's lives. So in one sense, the minister's wife should be friends with everyone in the congregation. At the same time, she obviously can't be close friends with everyone. Jesus left a good example for us in this. He had a large group of followers, a smaller group of twelve disciples, three with whom He had a closer friendship, and one whom He loved especially. Though we will not have followers and disciples like our Lord, we can still imitate Him in understanding the nature of friendship.

Proverbs says that we should choose our friends wisely, and the minister's family must exercise extra wisdom in this area. So here are a few observations from things I have learned over the years about friendships within the church.

First of all, as I said above, the minister's wife should be friends with everyone in her congregation. By this I mean that she should know their names, be friendly toward them, and genuinely interested in their lives. She should be approachable so that the ladies in her congregation feel free to call her if they need help or encouragement. She should participate in the life of the church, going to the wedding and baby showers, and other church-wide events as much as is possible, given her family duties and responsibilities. By getting to know the congregation, she will be a help to her husband by passing on information and questions that come up in her conversations. She may find out that someone is in real need of pastoral care, or that several families are having a squabble, or that the young people are watching dumb movies. This information will help her husband be a good pastor. I am not suggesting that the minister's wife is an undercover agent, but by living among the people her husband is pastoring, she can be a very big help to him.

When you move to a new church assignment, it is wise to take your time before you choose your friends. Get to know everyone. Be friendly to all the families and be cautious. Fast friends are not always the best friends. Every congregation will have its shy people and its outgoing people, and some may have an agenda that you are unaware of at first. Beware the people who are over-enthusiastic about you or your husband's ministry. It may be nice to hear such praise (for a change), especially if you have had experience with harsh criticism, but I warn you to be leery. People who are too lavish in their praise and eager to load you up with gifts may be setting themselves (and you) up for a crash.

Often those who were most supportive in the beginning turn out to be most critical later. A little cynicism and reserve will protect you from responding to such enthusiasm. Those who are too deferential may have you or your family on a little pedestal. You may be thinking, "Who? Us? But we are just normal!" But when those people find out you are just normal, they may react in a very spectacular way by leaving the church in a huff. Now I am not saying that the minister's wife should not accept gifts. But you should receive them with wisdom and keep a watch out for strings.

And I am not saying that everyone who gives you something has ulterior motives. Godly Christians are *supposed* to honor and give to the pastor and his family (1 Tim. 5:17). I am not such a hardened cynic as to set aside that scriptural requirement. But I am suggesting that those who are too lavish in their gift-giving to you may want something in return. And you don't want to give them the idea that they can be your near-and-dear friend if they spot you for a vacation or for dinner out or pay the down payment on your house. Like lobbyists in Washington, people sometimes give in order to have "access."

As you begin (or continue) your labors in your church, you will find women who are like-minded, the kind of women with whom you would like to be friends. As you begin to cultivate friendships, you may meet with resistance. If so, if someone doesn't seem to want to be friends with you for whatever reason, I encourage you to just let it go. Don't over-analyze it. To some it can be intimidating to be friends with the minister's wife. So don't take it personally. This comes with the territory.

You may naturally become friends with some of the elder's wives. They may have much in common with you, but don't expect them to have the same perspective that you do on the church or the ministry. I suggest that your friendship with another elder's wife not be centered on the church and its issues. Though your husbands are working together, it does not follow that you must discuss all the church business. In fact, that is a dangerous thing to do. Men are far better at disagreeing and debating as they work things out than women are. Men can continue to be friends and colleagues through some bumps, but their wives may not take it all as well. So steer clear of such things.

In all your friendships, be wise. If a friend asks why the elders made a certain decision, defer judgment. Unless your husband has told you what to say about a certain situation, it is best to say something like, "If you have a question about it, perhaps it would be best if you ask one of the men in leadership."

Be careful whom you confide in. Your husband should obviously be your nearest and dearest friend. Guard your lips. He may want you to be very mum about certain hardships. A careless word can be used against you later. Just imagine that what you say will be quoted to others. That should help you moderate what you say. We've all over-shared at one time or another. And when a friend has broken what you thought was a confidence, you should take it as a chastening from the Lord for your over-sharing and not as an opportunity to be annoyed with your friend.

In spite of these warnings, do not isolate yourself! If we just stayed home and never made friends with anyone, surely then we would not be hurt, right? Wrong. God has made us to need friends and to be a friend, so even though we should be careful, that does not mean we should be paranoid. If a close friend hurts you, then you have a Savior who knows all about it. Learn from your mistakes and press on. And cultivate friendships with wise women.

chapter 22

THICK SKIN

One of the things a minister's wife is going to need is thick skin. I think it is fairly safe to say that most pastors have to deal with criticism or controversy. We must expect it to come, and we must learn to handle it with grace and wisdom.

Let me start with a story. Years ago my husband wrote a conservative (of course) column for our local liberal (of course) newspaper. He gained quite a bit of notoriety in our small community for his pro-life stands and had enemies he had never met. One day I opened up our local newspaper and turned to the letters section to be greeted with a real stinker. As I recall, the full text of the letter was something like this: "Editor, Doug Wilson is a total idiot. Signed, Terry Lawhead." I felt as though someone had slugged me in the stomach. I really felt ill. I didn't like my husband being called names in the newspaper even though I had no idea who Terry Lawhead was.

It must have been a half hour or so before my husband got home. I showed him the letter, and he burst out laughing! He told me I should write in and say, "Editor, Terry Lawhead doesn't know the half of it. Signed, Nancy Wilson." I cut out that letter and kept it on the fridge for some time afterwards. It was sort of a turning point for me. In other words, I decided that if I was going to be in for a time with this husband of mine, I had better get hold of and hang on to a good sense of humor.

Some criticism is easy because it falls into the Terry Lawhead category. It comes from outside the church or from liberals who do not understand and cannot even engage in the argument. This is the kind that is easy to post on the fridge. But some criticism comes from fellow believers, even close friends who are members of the church, and this may require quite a different kind of processing to deal with biblically.

As I speak here about criticism, I need to specify exactly what I mean by the word. I do not mean brothers bringing constructive criticism to your husband. That can be a great blessing and help. It is a great privilege to have men who love the pastor and come with a gentle spirit to correct them if they need it, to ask questions, to give them feedback, etc. This is a sign of spiritual health in the church. It is an example of iron sharpening iron when men disagree in a humble yet invigorating manner. Rather, the kind of criticism I am discussing here is the kind that causes church splits and makes people angry. It stirs people up to choose sides. "There is one who speaks like the piercings of a sword, but the tongue of the wise promotes health" (Prov. 12:18). Yes, some words hurt us like the point of the sword.

Ministers are not the only people in the world who get criticized. Criticism is as old as dirt, as they say, and is common to many professions and callings. People complain about businesses and restaurants, doctors, teachers, police-men, building inspectors, senators, congressmen, newspa-per columnists, college presidents, parents, and children (to name a few). So a minister's wife should not fool herself into thinking this is unique to the ministry. It is always good to think about how many times you have heard something about another church or another minister and have listened, believed the report, and (horrors) even passed it on in casual conversation.

Years ago I was at a luncheon where some very sweet, dear Christian ladies were talking (very innocently) about a church and what they had heard about the recent "split." They were not being ugly about it; they were just sharing in-formation they had heard. Because our church had recently been on the receiving end of such chatter, I just couldn't bear to join in, so I turned away to visit with someone else. I don't want to be guilty of doing to other churches what has sometimes been done to ours. I'm thankful to have learned this lesson, and I hope I don't have to re-learn it.

But even though criticism is common as can be, we still (naively) expect to meet with better treatment from Chris-tian people, and so we may be caught off guard when it comes. But think about this for a minute. It was the *religious people* in Jesus' day who crucified him. It was not the pagans. Many of the martyrs were tortured and killed for the faith by fellow Christians who thought they were doing God a favor. (And by *Christians,* I am using the term to mean they professed to be followers of Christ, not followers of Buddha or Zeus.) So we really should not be surprised when fellow Christians, or even former friends, are the source of criticism or slander, though it is difficult to take. Remember that Judas was one of the Twelve, someone who had sat at the Lord's feet.

Now so far that is not very comforting. You may be thinking, "Thanks a lot." But actually the Scripture is full of comfort for us on this very topic. I just think we should clear away false perceptions first. We should not be surprised, and we should not feel alone. We are actually in good company. Just take a read through Hebrews 11 to be reminded what others have suffered before us. This is a great barrier to self-pity (which always gums everything up).

Remember God's sovereignty over all things. If your church is going through a hard time, you can look up. God is sanctifying, pruning, and growing His church. He allows hard times for our good and His glory. Many of you can look back on some of the hard times in your history and see how God worked them out for great good. So remember as you are on the receiving end of criticism or slander that God is ruling wisely over this too. It is ordained. This helps me to interpret each action rightly. God may not approve of the sinful attitude of the person saying the unkind thing, but He has sent it my way for my good. It is not willy-nilly. God does all things well. God is not doing this *to* me but *for* me. Now that is a biblical concept that will help you keep perspective.

There are different kinds of troubles. When you say *criticism,* you may mean someone didn't like the sermon or thinks the church should have more programs. Or maybe you mean that an ex-member is harassing the church by filing complaints with the city over building code or parking violations. There are different degrees of what we may call *criticism*. But whatever form it takes, we must look to the Scriptures to find our duties.

1 Peter 3:9 tells us that we should not return "evil for evil or reviling for reviling, but on the contrary blessing, knowing that you were called to this, that you may inherit a blessing." So that means we are to guard our hearts against bitterness or resentment toward the person doing the criticizing. We should be disposed to forgive those who wrong us (just in case they ever come asking for forgiveness). We should not backbite in return or snub them. We should look for opportunities to return good for evil. If you run into the wife of one of the troublemakers, you should be courteous. You do not have to pretend you are still the good friends you used to be, but you should treat her with kindness all the same. If she snubs you, well, you tried. "The discretion of a man makes him slow to anger, and his glory is to overlook a transgression" (Prov. 19:11).

We need to interpret our lives biblically. I commend the whole book of 1 Peter to you whenever you are faced with criticism. But here I will quote a couple of sections in particular. From 1 Peter 3:14–17:

> But even if you should suffer for righteousness sake, you are blessed. And do not be afraid of their threats, nor be troubled. But sanctify the Lord God in your hearts, and always be ready to give a defense to everyone who asks you

a reason for the hope that is in you with meekness and fear, having a good conscience, that when they defame you as evildoers, those who revile your good conduct in Christ may be ashamed. For it is better, if it is the will of God, to suffer for doing good than for doing evil.

And 4:14:

If you are reproached for the name of Christ, blessed are you, for the Spirit of glory and of God rests upon you. On their part He is blasphemed, but on your part He is glorified.

These verses require no commentary from me. God's ways are upside-down. Blessed when reproached? This is great news when you are feeling beat up from slander or criticism, whether it is from fellow Christians or from the world. Remember that if your husband is being faithful to the Lord, slander is a sign of blessing. I am amazed by the description of the blessing: *the Spirit of glory and of God rests upon you!* My husband calls it the Lord's promotion. Who would not welcome *that kind* of blessing?

But even when you try to view this from the Lord's perspective, it is still sometimes difficult to get your emotions to cooperate. So I find it helpful if I can put some practical application to work. This is what Jesus said about this subject (Mt. 5:11–12):

Blessed are you when they revile and persecute you, and say all kinds of evil against you falsely for My sake. Rejoice and be exceedingly glad, for great is your reward in heaven, for so they persecuted the prophets who were before you.

Here is more upside-down wisdom from God: we are to rejoice and be exceeding glad about lies and criticism. Rejoicing in the midst of slanderous accusations doesn't come naturally. In fact, it is more natural to get angry or to just curl up in a ball and get under the blankets! But that is a fleshly response, not a spiritual response. Look what the Lord wants us to do: He wants us to be exceedingly happy. Redouble your efforts to bless your husband in tangible ways. In order to do that, you have to be resting in God's promises and not worrying and fretting about the criticism and what the consequences of it might be.

A very hands-on way for me to do this is by throwing a party. I know this may sound weird, but it's more of God's upside-down way of doing things. We celebrate the arrival of the Lord's Day every Saturday night with our Sabbath feast. So, if my husband has been getting blasted in the newspaper or on the internet, I figure it is time to get a little bit more lavish with the menu. So I get more candy for the kids or I make a bigger dessert, or buy a better cut of meat and finer wine. This is my feeble attempt to do what Jesus says, to rejoice and be exceedingly glad. My emotions will follow along if I take this kind of action. Don't wait for the big whammy before you apply this. The more we apply it in the little things, the better equipped we are to apply it when the big stuff happens.

Over the years I have collected quite a number of quotations, and many of them (surprisingly) apply to this topic of criticism. Consider this one of Thomas Watson's: "Rather *be* wronged than *do* wrong." If someone is wronging your husband by bad-mouthing him, criticizing him in an ungodly manner, or passing on false information about him, think about this. It is better to be on the receiving end than to have such behavior on your own conscience. That is how Christ Himself was treated, and our husbands are not above their Master.

Another from Thomas Watson: "True grace may be shot at, but can never be shot through. Grace puts the soul into Christ, and there it is safe, as the bee in the hive, as the dove in the ark." We must remember where we are and who we are. And God has promised to preserve us.

Charles Spurgeon was familiar with slander: "The more prominent you are in Christ's service, the more certain are you to be the butt of calumny [slander]. I have long ago said farewell to my character. I lost it in the earlier days of my ministry by being a little more zealous than suited a slumbering age. And I have never been able to regain it except in the sight of Him who judges all the earth, and in the hearts of those who love me for my work's sake."

This is a very comforting position to take when your husband is being wronged. If God approves of his work, then let every man say what he will. As Spurgeon says, the more successful your husband's ministry, the more sure it is that he will be slandered. It is nothing new, and your husband is not the first faithful minister to receive such treatment.

I have no doubt that God uses criticism for our soul's good. He promises to use all for good in the lives of His children. Augustus Toplady knew this: "In a long sunshine of outward prosperity, the dust of our inward corruptions is apt to fly about and lift itself up. Sanctified affliction, like seasonable rain, lays the dust, and softens the soul, and keeps us from carrying our heads too high." Criticism can keep us humble, looking to Christ.

To quote another faithful saint, John Bunyan: "If I were fruitless, it mattered not who commended me, but if I were fruitful, I cared not who condemned." The presence of flattery or criticism is not the issue: the point is fruit. And if your husband is a fruitful man, it really doesn't matter who lets him have it. We should agree with Bunyan and not care about it. But this isn't always easy. The best ways to "not care" is to have a biblical view of criticism and to expect it. We want to have tender hearts and thick skins. We should be tender of others, tender toward God; but we should not be too tender of ourselves. Even so, God knows that a constant stream of the stuff can be wearisome. Psalm 31:20 addresses this: "Thou shalt hide them in the secret of thy presence from the pride of man: thou shalt keep them secretly in a pavilion from the strife of tongues." God can keep us in His pavilion, safe from the striving of wagging tongues. Isn't this a blessing? We must take advantage of His promise and go to His pavilion.

Finally, we must remember that criticism is actually healthy for us. Jesus has anticipated these things and has given us very specific directions. "Woe to you when all men speak well of you, for so did their fathers to the false prophets. But I say to you who hear: Love your enemies, do good to those who hate you, bless those who curse you, and pray for those who spitefully use you" (Lk. 6:26–28). When everyone is pleased with your husband, your souls may be in real danger. Keep these verses in mind as you handle criticism.

chapter 23

VULNERABILITY

One of the characteristics of the minister and his wife, by nature of the calling itself, is vulnerability. Each week the minister preaches to the congregation, opening himself up to them as he opens the Word. When he is counseling and teaching, he is giving himself away over and over again. He is a public figure, and any public figure is exposed to the censure and criticism of the world, and in the minister's case, it may be the censure and criticism of his own congregation.

This can be very difficult for the minister, but even more so for his wife. She knows her husband behind the scenes, how he labors in season and out of season for the sheep in the congregation, especially those who keep wandering off. The minister's wife sees the hours of preparation, the long days, and the late-night phone calls, the demands placed on her husband from many directions, and she naturally wants to be a protection for him.

But that is not exactly what we are called to do. The minister's wife should see herself as a source of refreshment, a line of supplies that keeps him going. But she can't protect him from the hazards of his own calling. If her husband were a soldier, she could not protect him from the hardships of war. If he were a doctor, she could not protect him from difficult patients or hard cases. So she must adapt to those things that come with the territory. Her husband is God's minister, and God appoints (and bestows) each congregational tangle, each counseling snarl, and every hardheaded parishioner who takes up an inordinate amount of time. When we remember that God has appointed each and every interruption, it is much easier to accept them with grace and gratitude.

But what about the criticisms and complaints? Does God appoint them as well? Of course He does. And the minister's wife must not let every complaint stumble her. I think that the wives can take the criticisms much harder than their husbands do, perhaps because we have an instinctive desire to protect and defend. Although the instinct itself is good, we must not protect in the wrong areas. This is God's territory, not ours. The wife cannot step between her husband and the criticism; she must get behind her husband and cheer him on, offering him the right kind of help, urging him to "Go, fight, win" and not "Run, hide, retaliate."

But this might be where the wife is severely tested. She may be tempted to offer bad advice that springs from wounded feelings ("How could they say such a thing about you after all you've done for them?") or make suggestions that betray a resentful heart ("He deserves to be excommunicated").

Being vulnerable is part of your calling as a minister's wife. Sometimes your friends leave for another congregation, and you may feel deserted and hurt. Don't worry about it. Let them go. Sometimes a family will disappear without a word, and they may be the family that your husband labored over in comforting and counseling through many hard times. Don't worry about it. Let them go. Sometimes a family leaves after stirring up dissension and trouble, or after spreading falsehoods about the elders or the minister or even you. Don't worry about it. Let them go. In this latter case, you can trust that God is pruning off the troublesome branches from the church. And in all cases, you can trust that God is pruning you. Take it all from His hand and trust Him. After all, this is His church, not yours.

When things like this happen, our fleshly impulse is to pull away, to pull back, to quit being so vulnerable to prevent future hurts. But this is actually the opposite of what the godly minister's wife should do. When people leave your church for another one, for whatever reason, you cannot hang on to them as though they belong to you. You should not be offended, though you may be tempted to be offended. If they were long-time friends and left without a thank-you or a goodbye, you must put the best spin on it. For them, they may view the church as something they choose like which grocery store they shop in. They don't realize how different your perspective is. The minister and his family view the church as their extended family (and many in the congregation view it this way as well). But some stay aloof so they can come and go as they please, never dreaming that you might feel sad to see them go. They are telling themselves one story, and you are telling yourself another. Let it go. Don't strive to prove a point. Don't embellish your story by attributing motives to them. Give them to God and ask Him to sort it out.

Of course you can't prevent missing those people who have left, whether they left for good reasons or not. You may always hold them in your heart. But the minister's wife may not allow herself to become resentful or bitter. This will simply make life uncomfortable, and why should we inflict misery on ourselves? Let the church leadership sort out the details, but don't let your flesh give way to hard feelings. As you let them go, let the hard feelings go too!

Here's a test to see if you are harboring resentment. Pray that God will bless these people who have left, who have spread lies, who have stirred up trouble. If the words get stuck in your throat, then you know you have resentment. The Bible says to return good for evil, to bless those who persecute you. So first confess the hard feelings, and then pray for God's blessings on them.

Next, ask God to give you an opportunity to do them good. I know of a couple who had been greatly harmed by the conduct of a fellow church member. Once when out to dinner, they noticed that their adversary was there in the same restaurant with his wife, so they asked the waitress to bring them the bill so they could pay for the couple's dinner. That is returning good for evil, and God always blesses that kind of behavior. If you are bitter, you are not free to act in such a manner.

If a minister is weighed down with troubles that come with his calling, that is all the more reason for his wife to be a weight-lifter rather than bringing more weight to his load. If you are rejoicing in the Lord, praying for your husband, and offering sweet counsel and refreshment, he will be greatly helped. But if you are also loaded down with his troubles, you will be too weak to be of much help. So cast your troubles on the Lord's shoulders, as He told us to do, and then you will be free to offer comfort to your husband.

Finally, don't let troubles affect the children. It's not their fault that so-in-so left the church in a huff. Rejoice around your table. Let your children participate in your comfort. They may be feeling sad about their own friends leaving the church. Maybe their friends even said rude things to them about their father. Set them an example of how to extend forgiveness. Pray with them. Make your home a place that is free from the fall out. Teach them the cost of opening your hearts and your home to others, and make sure they see that you are not looking for all the returns on your investments in this life.

Keep a sense a humor even in the hard times. Once when my daughter was in fifth grade and out at recess, one of her classmates surprised her by saying, "My pastor hates your dad! He says your dad is out drinking at the bars all the time!" Rachel's fifth-grade response was to fall on the ground laughing! That night at dinner she said something like, "So Dad, tell us about this other life you've been leading!"

If you can view these things as bumps in the road and not as major crashes, your family will be able to move forward more quickly. They will learn that this is not such a huge deal after all, that life goes on, that Mom is still having fun, and that Dad has her unswerving loyalty, support, and love. That is a lesson worth learning, and God teaches it to us by means of these troubles. He loves us, and He will never leave us or forsake us, though others will and do. If we embrace the troubles He brings, by grace, we will experience His blessings firsthand.

chapter 24

HOSPITALITY

One of the qualifications for a bishop (I Timothy 3:2) is that he must be hospitable, and that is one of the categories that concern many ministers' wives. Though I love having people over, and I love throwing a party, I often am thinking of all the people I wish I could have over for a meal. And I must confess that I have labored (with some success) to get out from under a load of (false) guilt over this for many years. Even when our church included only a couple hundred people, there was not much chance of having them all to dinner. And over the years it has grown to such numbers that it is out of the question.

Back when our church was very new and I was a very new wife of a very new minister, we had our first taste of friends leaving the church in an abrupt and unexpected manner. I was shocked. How could this be? One of the reasons they cited for leaving was that we had never had them over for a meal. I was stung, hurt, and crushed. How awful! If only I had invited them to dinner, they would have stayed in our church! But it didn't take long for my husband to help me sort this out. Think about this for a minute. That is an awful burden to place on any minister's wife, much less one that had only been at it for a few months! And just to make it more vivid in your mind, my husband's salary at that time was one hundred dollars a month (no joke) and the rest came in as a result of our prayers and the gracious provision of God.

I have learned over the years that people like that will never be pleased, and if I had invited them to dinner, no doubt something else would have come up in short order that would have displeased them, causing them to leave in spite of my hospitality. But that experience did leave me feeling a sense of responsibility that God had not put on me, and it took me a long time to get a sound perspective on hospitality. I was always wishing we could have more people over, but in reality, we were having truckloads of people over. One time I kept a tally, just to ease my mind. I was very surprised at the sheer numbers, but I was still not satisfied because I could think of many who had not been in our home.

Now many of you may not be able to relate to this at all. Perhaps you excel at hospitality and you've never had a twinge of concern about it. But many ministers' wives do feel a burden about hospitality. And if you think about it, hospitality should not be a burden but a joy.

I don't want to sound cynical, but be realistic about your own resources, gifts, obligations, and desires. You probably have a family, and they need your hospitality every night.

Not to mention your husband, the weary pastor who is dragging in the door after a long day of counseling, teaching, studying, etc. You don't want to be filling up his evenings when he needs to play with the kids and put his feet up.

Thankfully, God has given no requirement for pastors' wives to have each and every church member to dinner. But I still wish it were possible. I look around at the congregation and long to have them over. All of them. But I must be content with the finitude of my resources, time, and gifts.

But having dealt with any "false guilt," I do need to say that we must be hospitable people. Guilt is a poor motivator. God has given us a much better reason to share our homes and our tables. We honor and glorify Him when we feed people in His name. It is always better to give than to receive. It is spiritually healthy for us to extend ourselves and share and open our lives and our homes. It is a blessing.

Hospitality is not the same thing as entertainment. We don't have to have a home that looks like a page out of a catalogue. We don't have to break out the good china. The idea is fellowship and friendship.

When we were first married, Doug would invite his non-Christian college professors to dinner. We had a very small apartment furnished with second-hand furniture, and I can't remember what kinds of things I prepared for dinner. But I am grateful that it pushed me right out of my comfort zone. One of the professors we had over in those days is still in this community, and we see him from time to time. He continues to mention that meal that he shared with us over thirty years ago!

Our hospitality should include the alien, the stranger, the lonely, the widow, and the bereaved. We can't just have our close friends over week after week. God will bless these meals, however simple they may be.

But we must remember that hospitality, if it is going to be effective, must be an outworking of God's grace. We are going to need His strength and help to pull it off. And now I will include a story. When the kids were little, we had a large family in an RV pull up to our very small home. (When I say small, I am not joking. It was less than one thousand square feet.) My parents were visiting at the time, and we had made arrangements for this family to park their RV at the large home of one of the families in our congregation. But they didn't want to go there. They wanted to park at our house. It became apparent to me that they were staying for dinner . . . so I remember going into my kitchen and calling on the Lord, first for forgiveness, because I was not feeling very hospitable, and second for the grace to feed them cheerfully.

God did a wonderful thing that day. My mom sat and visited with the wife who was hungry for Christian fellowship, and my dad had a great time with the husband. Meanwhile the kids went out to play in the back yard. My youngest came in to complain that one of the boys was riding her trike, and I remember telling her that they might be angels that we were entertaining. (I remember her skeptical look!)

I made a huge vat of mac and cheese and the parents shuttled the kids in and out of our shower. And the whole thing was blessed, front to back, top to bottom. It was a spiritual success, which is why I remember it so well.

One more story. A few years prior to this, we were living in a small duplex. One of our friends, a young law student with a new wife, called to tell us that they were coming to dinner. They had no food, and they were hungry. At the time, my cupboards were a little thin, so I was scrambling to see what I could pull off to feed some extras. About that time my neighbor, a Korean woman whom Doug had led to the Lord, invited our daughter to come next door and help her make Korean food. When Bekah returned, she said that our friend was going to bring over a sample. I was expecting a small plate with a bite or two. But instead, she and her husband brought us several bowls and platters of different kinds of Korean food! We had a feast!

These stories just illustrate how faithful God is to enable us to open our homes and lives to feed people, even when it stretches us. We cannot expect to be faithful in hospitality apart from seeking God's help and grace. We should pray that God will enable us to be the kind of women who can throw an extra carrot in the pot if our husband calls to say he's bringing someone home for dinner.

We do not need to be intimidated by hospitality. God will meet us as we step out in faith. We are who we are. We don't have to pretend to be something impressive. And we can't have everyone to dinner; just those whom God sends.

chapter 25

SELF-EVALUATION

I thought it would be a good idea to take the last chapter to reflect on how "the minister's wife" is doing. Now I don't mean that I think we should get introspective about this in a gloomy way. That's not productive or fruitful. But from time to time we ought to step back and take a deep breath and give ourselves a look.

So how's that "helper thing" going anyway?

Our husbands are ministering in a wide variety of churches around the world. No two are alike (churches *or* ministers). Each of us is called to a particular man in a particular church in a particular time and place. And even though our churches may differ from one another, we have one central thing in common: we wives are all called to be *helpers* to our very own husbands/ministers. That help will be as individual as the men we are married to.

Because we are all married to ministers, we also have some other things in common: we are behind the scenes in lots of stuff going on in our churches. In fact, some of you may be up to your elbows in church programs and committees and Sunday school and ladies' prayer meetings and retreat planning and hosting Bible studies in your home and hospitality and counseling and on and on. You have an impressive load you are carrying.

I urge you to take a look at all the things you have been doing in the church (or in the community) this past year. Make a list. Then meditate on how (or whether) these things were a positive help to your husband. Consider the impact these activities have had on your children and on your home, *and on you*. How are *you* doing with all this? Are you feeling bogged down or rejuvenated? Are you constantly behind and peddling fast to catch up? Is each activity an overflow of joy, or is it something you just hunker down and do?

Some things are non-negotiable: you really should go to church each week! And of course there will be other things in that category, like feeding the family and doing the laundry. If those things have become drudgery to you, then it may be because of outside commitments that take too much of your time.

Now I don't want you to assume that I'm against the minister's wife being involved in church activities. That would be absurd. But neither am I against her *not* being overly involved. It all depends. Where does your husband need your help the most? What is he urging you to do? Have you done it? Or have you substituted something you wanted to do for something he wanted you to do? Have you substituted something you thought the congregation expected from you for something you wanted to do?

A minister's wife can feel pressure *to do* and *to be*. This pressure can come from the congregation or she can generate it all by herself. We can assume that our congregation is expecting certain things from us, and we can feel that we would be exposing our husband to criticism if we didn't do those things. ("The pastor's great, but his wife is a dud. Bummer.") So we rush in to fix it. But we shouldn't. We should pause and reflect a minute. Our mission is to help our husbands; it is not to help the congregation. And the sweet beauty of this is that if we are helping our husbands the way we should be, the whole congregation will be blessed.

If you have been maneuvered into doing things that you would have been wiser to say "no" to, your list of commitments may be looking like a large unwieldy pile of unfolded laundry. It's overwhelming. Where to begin? How will you ever get out from under this pile? At the same time, we do have gifts, and we should use them with all our might. But before we jump to any conclusions here, we ought to think about the big picture. Are we bestowing our gifts on the right people? Who are the primary recipients of these gifts of ours? Is our husband the primary beneficiary? How about the kids? How are they doing?

The minister's wife is like all other wives in this regard. You are called to love, respect, and obey your husband. You are called to love your kids and make a home for them. This is no mean feat. This takes courage, faith, strength, stamina, dedication, commitment, creativity, patience, diligence, endurance, love, and a whole lot of other stuff. It is more than a full-time calling, and it has enormous and eternal benefits.

If you find yourself looking around the congregation, seeing the total tonnage of needs out there, and feeling overwhelmed, then you need to pray for your pastor and elders. This is their job. You have your own congregation in your home. You are called to help your husband, to bring up your children, to guide your home, to bless your family. And if you focus on this, the overflow will naturally slosh out into the congregation. You just can't start out there. You have to start at home plate. That's where the action is for you.

Our husbands are in the thick of it. Remember that your husband's calling is not your calling. He is called to minister to the church, and you are called to minister to Him. *He is your calling.* If we are faithful and fruitful in this work of ours, our husbands will be built up and set free to minister God's Word and build up God's people. Keeping the home in order and feeding our people around the table is spiritual work indeed. Loving the kids and sitting at their ball games and helping them with their homework is spiritual. Keeping your husband's sock drawer full is spiritual. Having people to dinner is spiritual. And all these things take a lot of work. A minister who comes home to disorganized chaos, no dinner, and a frazzled wife is at a tremendous disadvantage; but the minister whose home is running on all cylinders has a tremendous advantage. We wives are the missing link here. It's our calling, our duty, and our job. We need to excel at this!

What has God called us to do? He wants us to be single-minded in following Him and His instructions. We are to be the kind of women who are committed to doing the duties God has laid out for us. Take a moment to think about these things. Now is a perfect time to do a check up, and remember to keep first things first. Love your kids. Respect your husband. Make your home a cheerful place. God will bless it!